Anglophone Expatriate Mothers Raising Biracial Children in Korea

Anglophone Expatriate Mothers Raising Biracial Children in Korea

A Pastoral Care Model

KAREN LOUISE KIM

WIPF & STOCK · Eugene, Oregon

ANGLOPHONE EXPATRIATE MOTHERS RAISING BIRACIAL CHILDREN IN KOREA
A Pastoral Care Model

Wipf & Stock
An Imprint of Wipf and Stock Publishers
199 W. 8th Ave., Suite 3
Eugene, OR 97401

www.wipfandstock.com

PAPERBACK ISBN: 978-1-5326-8983-3
HARDCOVER ISBN: 978-1-5326-8984-0
EBOOK ISBN: 978-1-5326-8985-7

Manufactured in the U.S.A.   OCTOBER 30, 2019

CONTENTS

LIST OF GRAPHS, TABLES
AND DIAGRAMS

PREFACE

THIS RESEARCH CONTRIBUTES THE experience of Anglophone women raising their biracial children to the growing literature on multiculturalism and international marriage in the context of Korea. Due to a number of differences in their immigration journey and sociocultural backgrounds, Anglophone women represent a different experience of migration and motherhood than women from other Asian nations who make up the majority of the current literature.

The question of experience is closely related to what it means for the mother to raise a citizen of a country that has clear in-group/out-group divides. The study takes a phenomenological qualitative approach with ten Caucasian women from Canada, America, and Australia who were residing in Korea while raising their biracial children with their Korean spouse.

Through the interviews with the participants, three major themes emerged relating to community, daily functioning in Korean society, and cultural and social identity. These themes were identified by the women as elements of their experience of cross-cultural motherhood in Korea. It is the dynamic of being included into a family of the destination country and how that influences an expatriate mother's experience of motherhood which is the focus of this research.

The pastoral care recommendations presented here propose additions to Carrie Doehring's approach to pastoral care by incorporating aspects of David Augsburger's understanding of intercultural pastoral care as well as acculturation theory. Firstly, I am advocating approaching care by listening to individual stories not only to understand the individual's immigration journey but how their values and priorities have been influenced by their experience of both cultures.

The model proposed here introduces an understanding of the caregiver as cogardener. In this sense the caregiver, as gardener, works alongside the careseeker, also respecting the individual skills they bring to the relationship, in order to work together to find adaptive solutions which will help the careseeker flourish within their particular new setting. In order to achieve this, I use the metaphor of a relational tree. This relational tree identifies a number of the support networks the women in the study identified, which are by no means exhaustive, but provide a starting point for the pastoral care of women parenting crossculturally in a way that may not necessarily be limited to the Korean context.

ACKNOWLEDGEMENTS

ANYONE WHO HAS GONE through the rigorous initiation process which is a PhD can testify that it can only be done in the context of community with the love, care, support, and sacrifice of many. There have been many professors who have encouraged and supported me along this journey, whom have inspired me in this undertaking for so many reasons. I would especially like to express my gratitude to my supervisor, Professor Soo-Young Kwon, who from the very beginning of this PhD journey saw my potential and the need for my research. I would like to thank my entire dissertation committee: Professors Jeung, You, Sohn, and Jang. Thank you for your generosity and sacrifice. I have learned so much and have been shaped professionally and personally by each of you. Joan Suwalsky, Sarah Son, Bridget McGregor, and Kelly Cross—thank you for giving your time, insights, and friendship. Your feedback and encouragement have been invaluable.

Seunghyuk David Kim, my inspiration and motivation. Thank you for being my "essential angel," behind the scenes. This dissertation is a product of your love, support, sacrifice, and prayers. I am so glad to have you as my partner in life. Thank you for being so faithful to our marriage vows and supporting me in my dreams at great cost. Finally, Joshua Yejun Kim, my monkey. In a very real way this research is for you. It is true that your arrival into this world put a pause on my PhD but it is also true that the adventure of motherhood you are taking me on is the inspiration for this thesis. And in conclusion: Romans 11:36.

Section 1

The Context: Fertile Grounds for Study

Chapter 1

INTRODUCTION

1.1 The Expatriate Experience of Mothering a Korean

ONE SUNNY AFTERNOON AT the end of a spring which had seen extremely high pollution levels, a mother ventured into the playground with her husband and preschooler. The playground was located in an apartment complex in East Seoul, South Korea, where they had been invited to have dinner at the house of the father's childhood best friend.[1] Having spent some time playing together, the father wandered off to another part of the playground to use his phone while the mother waited in line with their son to use the swing. After a moment, the pair drew the attention of two elementary school-aged girls who were at that time occupying both of the swings. Unconcerned with whether their comments would be understood and even less with the appropriateness of such comments, they began to talk between themselves in Korean about the "foreign English-speaking woman." Long accustomed to such comments from having lived in Korea for almost fifteen years, the Caucasian Australian mother only vaguely registered the childish chatter.

Within seconds, her three-and-a-half-year-old son's response changed that. With a fierceness rarely heard from him, he boldly shouted to the girls in fluent Korean slang, "Don't you dare speak about my mom that way!" Clearly taken aback, the older girls demanded to know the age of the boy, despite the fact that he was clearly much younger. Oblivious to the

---

1. Herein after to be referred to simply as "Korea."

offense and distress that they had caused the preschooler, they themselves had taken offense. From their perspective he had transgressed cultural and linguistic structures which dictate the way a younger person is required to address those older than themselves. Immediately the mother recognized the significance of this encounter in terms of its potential to shape the attitudes of all involved. Sensitive to her child's emotions, the mother also had little time to process and craft an appropriately articulate response in her second language. As a result, she feebly explained in Korean how the child's feelings had been hurt to hear them talking about his mother in such a way. Without apology and minimal acknowledgement, the girls lost interest in the exchange and the mother was left to hold her son close to comfort and reassure him. At that moment she felt torn between both pride in the fact that her son's love for her had caused him to be so protective but also regret and sadness that he had been placed in a situation where he had felt the need to defend her.

The incident above occurred to the writer and her son while this current research was being conducted. Its retelling and disclosure here serve two primary purposes. Firstly, and perhaps most importantly, it sets the stage for the material to be covered. The current study seeks to contribute the experience of Anglophone women raising their biracial children in Korea with their Korean spouse to the growing literature. The incident described above not only illustrates the phenomenon, but also gives some indication of the unique context within which it is emerging. Anglophone women represent a small and as yet underresearched part of a larger trend which is having a recognizable impact on Korean society.

1.2 Brief Overview of the Study

Multiculturalism in Korean society is a growing topic of discussion in government, academic, and colloquial circles. Diverse factors such as Korean discourses of homogeneity, the particular form of patriarchy present in Korean society, a rapid influx of international brides, an aging population, and a dramatically shrinking birth rate have all converged in recent decades to make it one of the most pertinent issues currently facing Korean society. In his discussion of Korea's myth of homogeneity, Kevin Cawley cites numerous Korean and nonKorean sources that similarly claim that as an increasingly multiracial and multiethnic society, "multiculturalism is one of the most critical issues in South Korea today."[2] From the outset, the above incident demonstrates one example of the impact of these various ideologies and discourses as they are played out in the playground in contemporary Korea. More specifically, it also introduces aspects of attention, language, and social acceptance which emerged in the responses of participants in the present study. Uncovering the way these discourses were experienced was the primary reason for selecting a phenomenological methodology for the study.

The second reason for introducing the research with this account is to intentionally position the writer in relation to the phenomenon being addressed. After conducting ten semistructured interviews focusing on the expatriate woman's experiences of motherhood in Korea, a number of other illustrations could have been chosen, many of them perhaps much more positive than the example given. Describing the researcher's experience with the trend under study is a recognized starting point of a phenomenological analysis method adapted from Moustakas.[3] As will be discussed at various points in the following chapters, the researcher's position within the community under study had implications for the participant's recruitment and interviews as well as the data analysis stage of the research.

Presented here are the findings of a phenomenological study of ten Caucasian women from Canada, America, and Australia residing in Korea with their Korean spouses and their dual-citizen children. As will be outlined in this chapter, not only does Korea prove to be a unique case study of international marriage and migration, the majority of the research addressing this trend has focused primarily on the experience of marriage migrants to Korea from other parts of Asia. The purpose of the study is to contribute to the discourse on multiculturalism in Korean society by offering a more complex description of the priorities and experiences in relation to the acculturation and cultural integration of immigrant women who are raising their children in Korea. The intention of such a description is to provide suggestions and recommendations for pastoral counseling and care applications.

This exploration of the experiences of Anglophone expatriate mothers in Korea is based on two premises which are developed from the literature review. Firstly, there is the assumption that due to a number of differences in their immigration journey as well as their sociodemographic and

---

2. Cawley, "Back to the Future," 155.

3. Creswell, *Qualitative Inquiry*, 193.

cultural backgrounds, the women in this study will represent a different experience of migration and motherhood than the women from other Asian nations. Furthermore, each woman's experience and acculturation is heavily influenced by her status as both a marriage immigrant, a parent raising a child in the destination culture, and a member of a family of citizens of that country. Although not addressing the specific family dynamic detailed in this research, acculturation theorist Marc Bornstein does recognize that the parent-child relationship is an "important domain where the dynamics of acculturation play out."[4] More generally, immigration status and purpose, alongside individual and contextual factors such as destination and origin cultures, are all variables of immigration which Bornstein argues influence acculturation.[5]

The question of experience is closely related to what it means for the mother to raise a citizen of a country which has clear in-group/out-group divides. It is the dynamic of being included into a family of the destination country which is of interest. The assumption is that being a member of the family of the destination country is a different acculturation experience than parenting as an expatriate with an expatriate spouse. In other words, "what does it mean to raise a Korean citizen in the largely homogeneous Korea, when you aren't Korean yourself?" Both the meaning this holds for the women and how they navigate it will vary depending on their priorities and their experience of acculturation.

Chapter 7 proposes an approach to pastoral care after considering the findings of the phenomenological study conducted with ten Anglophone expatriate mothers raising their biracial children in Korea in light of the discussion of Doehring's approach to pastoral care and acculturation theory in chapter 2. Following on from the findings in this study, this book proposes a feminist influenced *critical correlation* method of pastoral counseling as described by Carrie Doehring and others, which brings the perspectives of different disciplines into dialogue together.[6]

As a result of the themes which emerged from the participant's responses, what is being proposed here is an acculturation assessment in addition to the cultural and social assessment of a person seeking pastoral care or the "careseeker" as Doehring's model proposes. In other words,

4. Bornstein, "Specificity Principle," 10.

5. Bornstein, "Specificity Principle," 6.

6. Poling and Miller (1985), Browning (1991), Doehring (1999), and Ramsay (1998) in Doehring, "Developing Models," 9.

when contemplating the pastoral care of an expatriate mother in Korea, it is necessary for the caregiver to give due attention to the various ways her acculturation is influencing her experience. This is achieved by elaborating on David Augsburger's theories of interpathy and the development of a metaphor of a relational tree. This deepens the assessment of the individual's support network by factoring in her access to different support communities and the way in which her connection to a Korean family has influenced her experience, perspective, practices, and needs. The metaphor of a tree also gives recognition to the fact that it is a dynamic and changing process.

It is anticipated that the application and extension of this model of pastoral care may be adapted for use when providing pastoral care for a wide range of expatriates outside of the immediate Korean context. With increased global movement, which Bornstein and Constable outline in detail,[7] it is increasingly likely that pastors will find themselves with expatriates in their congregation regardless of their location. As a result, it is important for pastors to consider how various factors have influenced not only the careseeker's experience of immigration and their access to resources, but also their priorities and rational behind acculturation. Just as Doehring's approach begins with listening to the narratives about the careseeker's "self, family, community, and culture,"[8] what is needed is to first hear their stories.

In the case of the expatriate mother in particular, the conversations Doehring endorses involve listening to stories of what aspects of both cultures have become significant and important to her and the priorities she has for passing these on to her children. The participants in the study were not only proactive decision-makers, they had a carefully thought-out rationale for the decisions they had made. At the very least they had experimented and had either incorporated or dismissed what worked for them and their situation. Although this may initially sound like an autonomous process, the decisions take place within the context of community on the basis of experiences with her husband, his family, Korean society more generally, and relationships from her family and culture of origin. This is also reflected in the tree motif. Before elaborating on the themes and application further, it is first necessary to articulate the phenomenon under study. This book proposes that Anglophone women bring their values and immigration journey

7. Bornstein, "Specificity Principle"; Constable, *Global Stage*.
8. Doehring, "Developing Models," 166.

into their motherhood experience in the unique context of Korea, which has implications for their acculturation and pastoral care.

1.3 Marriage Migration in Korea: Trends and Research

In order to explore the question of how Anglophone women understand and experience motherhood within the context of Korean society it is first necessary to examine the trend of international marriage in Korea and the context in which it is occurring.

Without a doubt, the growth in international marriages in Korea has received a lot of interest in both popular and academic sectors. Many report that the trend of marriage immigrants gained popular attention in the 1990s and 2000s with the influx of ethnically Korean women from China marrying Korean men becoming the first to gain national coverage.[9] Interestingly, one of the major qualitative studies on this phenomenon was conducted by an American author. Caren Freeman published a particularly insightful study with a focus on the female Korean diaspora from China known as *Chosŏnjok*.[10] Freeman highlights the implications of her ethnographic research as facilitating an understanding of the "the historical precedents of what has become a steadily growing and contentious phenomenon in South Korea today."[11]

She describes the early stages of the international marriage phenomenon in Korea, claiming that these marriages to *Chosŏnjok* women in 1990 were the earliest examples of these kinds of international marriages which were facilitated by a government-led campaign to find suitable spouses for rural bachelors. This history and development is consistent with what Korean writers have also described.[12] However, it appears this is not the full picture of the trend. As Nora Hui-Jung Kim claims, even though the *Chosŏnjok* brides were the first to draw national attention, Japanese brides arriving as a result of marriages arranged by the Unification Church in the 1980s and 1990s were actually the first wave of international marriage with female spouses in Korea.[13]

9. Kim, "Naturalizing Korean Ethnicity," 193.

10. Freeman, "Marrying Up."

11. Freeman, "Marrying Up," 3.

12. Chung and Yoo, "Support Centers"; Yang, "Multicultural Families"; Bélanger et al., "Ethnic Diversity."

13. Kim, "Naturalizing Korean Ethnicity," 193.

Some scholars writing in relation to international marriages in Korea have also recognized a trend of Western men married to Korean women which preceded the current wave of international marriages.[14] This is supported statistically with Korean scholars noting the drastic increase in the number of foreign women married to Koreans which jumped from 46.4 percent of all international marriages in 1994 to 79.3 in 1996, showing the point where international brides began to far exceed the number of international grooms.[15] This suggests that it is the female spouses from parts of Asia and China in particular who were responsible for this shift.

The phenomenon of international brides expanded in the mid 2000s to include a significant number of women from countries within Southeast Asia as diverse as "the Philippines, Vietnam, Indonesia, Thailand and Cambodia."[16] Statistics show that "the percentage of total marriages that involve a foreign spouse increased threefold over the four-year period between 2001 and 2005, from 4.6 to 13.6 per cent."[17]

The latest statistics on marriage and divorce have actually found the number of cases of international women married to Koreans overall to be slowly decreasing at a consistent rate since its peak in 2005.[18] However, marriages with a foreign spouse still accounted for 7 percent of the total marriages in Korea in 2015.[19] Even though the overall trend in international marriages appears to have peaked, it also seems to have developed into other trends which could foreseeably have a long-lasting impact on Korean society.

Adding even greater significance to the trend, despite its decline, is the rate of immigrant mothers giving birth. Bornstein notes that lowering birth rates and lengthening life expectancy in developed nations will lead many of these economies to increasingly rely on the contributions of immigrants.[20] Statistics show that in the specific context of Korea, the birth rate of children in multicultural families will also have a growing impact. Although distinguished by nationality, the rate of immigrant mothers

14. Lee et al., "International Marriages"; Kim, "Marriages of Asian Women"; Abelmann and Kim, "Failed Attempt."

15. Yang, "Multicultural Families," 52.

16. Kim, "Naturalizing Korean Ethnicity," 193.

17. Lee et al., "International Marriages," 166.

18. Statistics Korea, "Marriage and Divorce."

19. Statistics Korea, "Marriage and Divorce."

20. Bornstein, "Specificity Principle," 30.

giving birth has both increased in recent years and stayed at a consistent level in comparison to the overall number of births in Korea. Immigrant women have been reported as recently as 2015 to represent 4.9 percent of women having live births in Korea, a rate which is remaining somewhat consistent.[21] There has also been a reported increase in the number of multicultural children being born. From 2006 to 2008 the number of children born into multicultural families in Korea went from 25,000 to 58,000.[22] Furthermore, over half of these children were born toward the end of this period,[23] which indicates the trend of growth will continue. Demographic researchers have predicted that if these trends remain consistent, then "more than one in nine children" in Korea could represent a multicultural heritage by 2020.[24]

The way children in multicultural families are raised and socialized is going to have a significant impact on Korean society in the future. According to one New York Times article, the birth of these multicultural children is "confronting this proudly homogeneous nation with the difficult challenge of smoothly absorbing them."[25] These predictions are somewhat supported by recent statistics which show that the number of Korean citizens holding dual citizenship is increasing every year, jumping from 15,235 in 2011 to 85,965 in August 2017.[26] Significantly, in Korea exceptions allowing a person to hold dual citizenship are only made to those who receive dual citizenship through birthright, have married Korean citizens or are over sixty-five years old and want to revive their Korean citizenship.[27] Therefore, marriage immigrants and their children can reasonably be understood as an important factor leading to the increase in numbers of dual citizenship. This indicates the social impact that the trend of international marriage is having and will continue to have on Korean society.

Although there is a demonstrable and significant trend of international marriage migration occurring in Korean society, Anglophone women from Western countries marrying Korean men represent a small portion of this phenomenon. More recent immigration statistics from 2015 show that

21. Statistics Korea, "Vital Statistics of Immigrants."
22. Chosun Ilbo, "Right Approach to Care."
23. Chosun Ilbo, "Right Approach to Care."
24. Fackler, "Baby Boom."
25. Fackler, "Baby Boom."
26. Chung, "Dual Citizenships."
27. Chung, "Dual Citizenships."

of the 14,677 marriages between Korean men and non-Korean women, only 577 were American citizens, whereas 12,299 originated from other parts of Asia.[28] In 2011, the percentage of women from Western regions such as Europe and North America was approximately 1.7 percent of the total women migrants in Korea in that period.[29] Therefore, the number of Western women marrying Korean men is demonstrably a much smaller part of the overall trend of international marriages in Korea.

As well as marrying Korean men less often than do women from other Asian countries, other statistics from Korea Statistical Information Service (KOSIS) demonstrate that Anglophone women are also sojourning in Korea as spouses in smaller numbers as well.[30] Looking at statistics of visa holders alongside annual statistics of international marriage gives a somewhat longer-term context of this trend which suits the purposes of this current research. Residency, more than marriage statistics alone, is a better indication of the number of multicultural couples settling in Korea with the possibility of raising children there. Statistics from KOSIS most recently updated in August 2017 covering the period of 2012–2016, detail the number of immigrants residing in Korea on various visas offered to spouses of Korean nationals (F-2-1, F-5-1, F-6-1) and those raising Korean nationals (F-6-2) according to country of citizenship.[31] Of the 152, 374 visa holders in this category, women represent the clear majority at 128, 518.[32] Interestingly, the numbers from Anglophone Western nations do not follow this trend where women are represented in larger numbers. There is a reversal in these Western nations with men far outnumbering the women (see table 1).

28. Son, *National Identity*, 632.

29. Park et al., "Social Constructions," 114.

30. Statistics Korea, "Marriage Migrant."

31. Statistics Korea, "Marriage Migrant."

32. Statistics Korea, "Marriage Migrant."

Table 1. Number of Anglophone Spousal Visa Holders by Country and Gender in 2016

Country	Male	Female
United States	2,537	817
Canada	1,112	206
United Kingdom	766	76
Australia	319	64
New Zealand	216	24
Ireland	106	11

Consistent with the marriage statistics, at a little less than 1 percent of total women visa holders, women from Anglophone countries do represent a much smaller percentage of international marriage immigrants residing in Korea when compared to women from Asian countries. It does not, however, automatically follow that their presence and experience of child-rearing should be dismissed from the discussion of multiculturalism as it is unfolding in Korea. On the contrary, given the potentially greater cultural differences experienced by Western migrants, their understanding and ne-gotiation of Korea's homogeneity whilst raising their children there could provide valuable insights for the ongoing dialogue.

1.4 Previous Studies on International Marriage in Korea

Although a number of people have written about the growing phenomenon of marriage migration in Korea, with some even touching on the topic of raising children there, most have focused on the brides from other Asian nations. This is understandable given that, as previously mentioned, the ma-jority of the female marriage migrants are coming from this region. Korean academics have themselves noted that the majority of recent Korean schol-arship on the issue of immigration has focused on the international brides and their "unilateral acculturation toward Korean cultural patterns."[33] Fur-thermore, in terms of acculturation, one study found that the Asian spouse's "retention of Asian cultural collectivism contributes to ethnic Asian bride's

33. Oh et al., "Asian Cultural Collectivism," 29.

satisfaction in Korean society."[34] In other words, the findings suggest that similarities in cultural background made acculturation easier, which contributed to levels of life satisfaction. Implying what could be understood as assimilation, the authors also claimed that a woman's level of satisfaction with her life in Korea increased as her understanding and "attachment" to Korean traditions and cultural norms deepened.[35]

Qualitative studies on interethnic and interracial families' use of government-initiated programs in South Korea have also been conducted, although yet again, they have focused on marriage immigrants from non-Western countries. One example is a narrative study by H. Chung and Joan P. Yoo which examined marriage immigrants use of the Multicultural Family Support Centers that have emerged as a result of the Multicultural Family Support Act of 2008.[36] None of the ten brides interviewed were native English speakers, although one participant was from outside of Asia.[37] This may, however, be reflective of the fact that Western women neither participate in significant numbers nor consistently in these official programs when compared to the women representing other countries throughout Asia. From the author's experience of being involved with the Seodaemun Multicultural Center from 2011 to 2014, which included taking classes and participating in combined events with centers from other locations across Seoul, she was only able to meet two other Westerners (Americans) during that time. It not only demonstrates that Anglophone women are underrepresented in the current literature, but also raises the question of what strategies and programs they are utilizing in their experience of mothering in Korea.

Exploring the extent to which the Western woman raising her child in Korea both incorporates her own traditions and adapts her mothering style to the wider social context offers a unique contribution to the discussion on multiculturalism in Korea. One literary review focusing on immigrant spouses identified the difficulties these families face particularly in relation to cultural differences, conflict between the spouses, as well as between the daughter-in-law and mother-in-law.[38] A recent study even compared incorporation policies directed at North Koreans resettling in South Korea

---

34. Oh et al., "Asian Cultural Collectivism," 23.

35. Oh et al., "Asian Cultural Collectivism," 23.

36. Chung and Yoo, "Support Centers," 241–42.

37. This participant was from Peru. See Chung and Yoo, "Support Centers," 244.

38. Chung and Yoo, "Support Centers," 241.

with those directed to foreign brides.[39] The issue has also been approached in Korean scholarship from many different disciplines. Firstly, Yeong-mee Lee[40] contributed a feminist theological reflection on the trend of female marriage migrants in Korea which will be discussed and evaluated together in relation to other feminist theology in chapter 2. Others have approached the subject from the field of nursing and mental health.[41] Both of these approaches have implications for the current study.

Along with the theological exploration of marriage and migration in Korea, which will be discussed in the following chapter, studies on the immigrant spouse's mental health are also of particular interest to the current research. A number of studies have been conducted exploring mental health through the lens of multiculturalism. In relation to multicultural issues and parenting, one study has researched the effect of the mother's perception of discrimination, maternal depression, and general parenting behaviors on the psychological adjustment of the adolescent children of these families.[42] Another has looked at the impact of differences in family values between a non-Korean wife and a Korean husband on depression in foreign wives, evaluating the effectiveness of social support.[43] Yet another has examined the impact of responses to ethnic discrimination on measures of selfrated health among marriage migrants in South Korea.[44] None of the findings of these studies are surprising, showing a correlation between discrimination, real or perceived, and negative outcomes in adjustment and wellbeing of multicultural families. These are important contributions to the discussion of mental health, multiculturalism, and marriage migration in Korea. However, once again, the discussion is limited to women from other parts of Asia and fails to shed light on the experience of Anglophone women with Western backgrounds who are married to Korean men and residing with their families in Korea.

One study of marriage migrant women in Busan, a southern coastal city of Korea, focused on the acculturation stress the women experienced. The study recommended that educational programs designed to develop

39. Kim, "Naturalizing Korean Ethnicity."

40. Lee, "Ruth and Marriage."

41. Kim et al., "Predictive Factors"; Kim, "Social Integration"; Im et al., "Acculturation Stress."

42. Chung and Lim, "Marriage Immigrant."

43. Won and Kim, "Family Values."

44. Kim et al., "Fair Treatment."

coping mechanisms and social support, among other things, were necessary to enhance the mental health of marriage migrants.[45] This study was
limited to survey responses of women from other parts of Asia. Furthermore, in their exploration of acculturation stress, they were seeking to
understand the "psychological symptom of the inability of immigrants to
integrate into the mainstream of the host society."[46] The participant's responses were framed by questions addressing predetermined domains and
categories which included coping resources, and as a result, limited their
opportunities to articulate their needs and resources for themselves. This
study proposes not only that women from Anglophone countries will have
a different experience of immigration and acculturation in Korea, but that
a phenomenological qualitative study is the most appropriate avenue to
explore these differences. As a result, this work will take this methodological approach in order to contribute the experience of Anglophone women
parenting interculturally as an expatriate in the context of Korea to the current literature.

1.4.1 Literature Review of Multiculturalism in Korea

Before the significance of the experience of Anglophone expatriate mothers
raising their biracial children in Korea can be discussed, it is important to
examine the discourse surrounding multiculturalism in Korea. Discourse
has been understood as "an institutionalized way of talking that regulates
and reinforces action and thereby exerts power."[47] It is from this understanding of discourse that the concepts of multiculturalism, homogeneity,
and patriarchy are being used and understood in this research.

The Korean context of multiculturalism in which immigrant women
are raising their children is a complex discourse influenced by notions of
both homogeneity and patriarchy alongside other social factors. This is
contrasted with the context of Western nations such as America, Canada,
and the United States. These countries "are distinguished in having long
histories as immigrant-receiving societies."[48] This is to the extent that they
have been categorized together as a form of multicultural society "where

---

45. Im et al., "Acculturation Stress," 497.

46. Im et al., "Acculturation Stress," 498.

47. Link cited in Jäger and Maier, "Theoretical and Methodological Aspects," 35.

48. Washbrook et al., "Development of Young Children," 1591.

the majority of citizens are immigrants or descendants of immigrants."[49] In this form of multicultural society, "multiculturalism itself has been the basis of nation building or the principle of citizenship."[50] This contrasts with the discourse of homogeneity in Korea where, as will be developed further in the following sections, ethnicity is intimately linked to nation building and citizenship. Due to the particular narrative of homogeneity, race becomes an important part of the experience of multiculturalism in Korean society.[51] In exploring the meaning that the experience of raising a multiracial child in Korea has for the women in this study, the core question is how the women understand the power that these various discourses exert over their experience.

Due to the country's trends of increasing international marriage and low birth rates, a number of Korean scholars have written about the rhetoric of multiculturalism, particularly looking at areas of policy development and the history of the trend. Hyunah Yang has argued that a unique and complicated form of multiculturalism has formed in Korea. She takes a socio-legal approach to examine the ways in which legislation has been used to accommodate "a form of migration" which has led to the particular form of multiculturalism that is currently emerging in Korea.[52] Accordingly, there have been two dominant trends in the discussion of Korean multiculturalism in the literature.

Firstly, as indicated previously, there have been a large number of articles in a wide variety of disciplines discussing the wave of Southeast Asian brides entering Korea. Yang claims that Korea's multiculturalism has been widely criticized for its emphasis on cultural assimilation of the migrants, particularly in relation to the family.[53] Also within this first category of literature, concerns have been expressed over the women's objectification, with more recent feminist research focusing on the level of agency the women themselves exhibit in their decision to migrate to Korea through marriage.[54]

49. Yang, "Multicultural Families," 55.

50. Yang, "Multicultural Families," 55.

51. See Cawley, "Back to the Future"; Son, *National Identity*.

52. Yang, "Multicultural Families," 57.

53. Yang, "Multicultural Families," 57.

54. See Freeman, *Making and Faking Kinship*; "Marrying Up"; Jung, "Let Their Voices"; "Constructing Scales"; Lee, "Trafficking in Women?"; Robinson, "Marriage Migration"; and also Constable, *Global Stage*, and *Cross Border Marriages* in relation to the Mail Order Bride phenomenon more generally.

The second trend in the discussion of multiculturalism reflects a general criticism of the emphasis that policies place on multicultural families with a non-Korean wife, while neglecting families that don't fit this category, as well as the growing number of migrant laborers in Korea.[55] Geon Soo Han goes so far as to argue that "current discourses and concerns on multiculturalism in Korea are mere political rhetorics and slogans, not the constructive and analytical concepts for transforming a society."[56] Others have noticed this same sentiment in other scholarship claiming that "the government driven discourse has swept through the country extremely rapidly, is excessively ambitious, and is too abstract. In fact, the policies and programs tend to be mere displays for showing off government achievements."[57] This further demonstrates not only a need for a deconstruction of this particular narrative of multiculturalism in Korea, but also the need for a description of how it is lived experientially in the lives of those who are the subjects of this discourse. Beyond discussing notions of "Multiculturalism as rhetoric," it is important to ask the marriage immigrants themselves what being a multicultural family means to them and their families personally.

Various factors, such as marriage introduction services and the reasons they were established, have contributed to the particular narrative of multiculturalism which has emerged in Korea. Indeed, the issue of immigrant brides is not unique to Korea or even to Asia. Nicole Constable has been an active writer from the feminist perspective on the phenomenon of Asian Mail Order Brides in America.[58] More specifically, connections and similarities have been identified between female marriage migration in Korea with Taiwan and even Japan based on their similar social trends of plunging birthrates, aging populations, and the lack of spouses, especially for rural bachelors, as native women seek career opportunities in urban cities.[59] Aside from these social concerns, Korea is distinguished as an immigrant-receiving nation due to its homogeneous self-understanding.

---

55. See Park et al., "Social Constructions"; Kim, "Global Migration"; Ahn, "Racial Project."

56. Han, "Multicultural Korea," 32.

57. H. Kim cited in Kim, "Daughters-in-Law of Korea?," 8.

58. Constable, *Global Stage*; *Cross Border Marriages*.

59. See Bélanger et al., "Ethnic Diversity"; Jones and Shen, "International Marriage"; Kim and Oh, "Multicultural Contention."

1.4.2 Homogeneity in the Context of Korea

Korea's notion of homogeneity has been a large contributing factor to the current narratives of multiculturalism which have emerged in Korea and has implications for the acculturation of immigrants. The notion of multiculturalism has been understood to be highly contextual, dependent on the local and political climate of a given country.[60] Many Korean scholars have recognized that the particular form of nationalism and the notion of an ethnically homogeneous nation state founded in the claim that Koreans are "descendants of a common ancestor" gained strength as a challenge to Japanese colonial attempts in Korea in the early twentieth century.[61] This concept of "purity of blood" has also been "understood exclusively as the paternal line."[62] Yang argues that the uniqueness of the form of multiculturalism developing in Korea lies in the fact that the majority of Koreans identify with the idealized homogeneity of this discourse and the expectation for the immigrant spouse to adapt to their Korean family, rather than a multiculturalism in which migrants form a "discrete ethnic community" as in other countries.[63] The result is a form of multiculturalism where cultural conflict and difference are being negotiated in the home within a family setting.[64] It is the acknowledgement that multiculturalism is in many ways negotiated in the context of the family, which is the reason that the focus of this study is the participants' experiences of motherhood. Even so, the way multiculturalism is played out in Korean society outside of the family is also influenced by this myth of homogeneity, which is navigated by multicultural families, especially those consisting of a Western mother.

The impact of this myth of homogeneity on multiculturalism can be seen in the work of many scholars. Timothy Lim claims that "the discourse of Korean homogeneity, based on a hitherto unyielding conflation of race and ethnicity, made/makes possible the near-total exclusion of 'non-Koreans' from membership in Korean society."[65] Exploring the issue of social exclusion of rural brides was even the topic of one particular study.[66]

60. Modood cited in Beckett and Macey, "Race, Gender and Sexuality," 310. This is especially evident in the context of Korea.

61. Cawley, "Back to the Future," 150–51.

62. Kim, "Daughters-in-Law of Korea?," 9.

63. Yang, "Multicultural Families," 56–57.

64. Yang, "Multicultural Families," 57.

65. Timothy Lim, "Rethinking Belongingness," 53.

66. Kim and Shin, "Immigrant Brides," 2008.

Furthermore, Mary Lee explores how the notion of "blood purity" and imagined homogeneity in Korean society has, through the construction of "othering," not only led to the discrimination of multicultural people with one Korean parent, but is the result of racial and gendered politics.[67] Although Lee explores the experience of "Amerasians" and their relationship to Korean society, her definition of "Amerasians" is limited only to the children with an American father and a Korean mother, a phenomenon she sees as a result of America's involvement in the Korean war.[68] Similar gendered politics are potentially at play when the mother is non-Korean, although it is important to consider how an expatriate mother's experience of mothering in Korean society is influenced by the othering of herself and her child and the potential challenges this may present to her. It appears necessary to contribute to the discussion of multiculturalism in Korea the perspective of what it means to raise a Korean citizen, when you are not one and your child may not be socially accepted as one.

Choong Soon Kim argues that, contrary to this perception of Korea as a homogeneous society, Korea has a rich heritage of multiculturalism and even multicultural marriage.[69] Hyun Choe also makes strong claims that as a result of multicultural marriages, "the myth of South Korea's ethnic and cultural homogeneity is crumbling."[70] Choe argues that a change in ideology and civil consciousness is needed, among other things, in order for Korea to "utilize its growing plurality as a driving force for social development."[71] The book *Voices of Foreign Brides*[72] seems to be a step in this direction as Kim approaches the issues of both discourse and legislation in relation to multiculturalism from an anthropological perspective. One reviewer summarizes Kim's work as the investigation into "the ways in which multiculturalism is conceptualized, its future, and how multicultural policies reflect the needs and desires of foreigners, particularly foreign brides."[73]

Although promising and useful, the voices that Kim presents are once again the brides from other Asian countries, even though he himself has a Caucasian daughter-in-law. Despite including himself as being a member

67. Lee, "Mixed Race Peoples," 56.
68. Lee, "Mixed Race Peoples," 57.
69. Kim, *Voices of Foreign Brides*.
70. Choe, "South Korean Society," 123.
71. Choe, "South Korean Society," 123.
72. Kim, *Voices of Foreign Brides*.
73. Delaney, "Voices," 149.

of a "multicultural family" his is clearly not the kind of multicultural family he is discussing. This discussion of multiculturalism in the Korean context is again limited to a very narrow field of a particular group of immigrant brides. In exploring multiculturalism from the perspective of women from these nations, the question of what multiculturalism means to families with an Anglophone mother and wife is again left unanswered.

There are also other limitations to Kim's work. Indeed, although it opens a discussion for deconstructing the myth of homogeneity in Korea, a major criticism of *Voices of Foreign Brides*, according to Robert Delaney, is its failure to examine the "superstructure" of governmental factors which he argues oversee and assign roles to the foreign brides.[74] Delaney also cites government documents which he shockingly claims refer to the women as "an object that can be used to resolve Korea's low birth, aging society crisis."[75] He further comments how the social protection of these women "is linked to how they fulfilled their role as mothers instead of to their existence as human beings."[76] I have argued elsewhere that in order to assimilate foreign brides, their gender is being construed in particular ways which conform to Korea's form of patriarchy, namely through the roles of wife, daughter-in-law and mother.[77] In other words, Korean society is able to tolerate the onslaught of multiculturalism to its notion of a homogeneous society to the extent that the women themselves conform to these roles, resulting in as minimal social disruption as possible while producing "good" Korean citizens. Of course, this is not limited to Korea. American scholars have also noted, "Gender distinctions, however distorted and unjust, remain the backbone of social order, undergirding not just society's reproductive arrangements, but plainly, the way people see and understand the world."[78] Hence, gendered roles are part of the context in which immigrant brides find themselves in Korea. Although important in demonstrating the influence that a combination of homogeneity, patriarchy, and a low birth rate have in the narrative of multiculturalism which has emerged in Korea, the "voices" of Western women and how they are experiencing or even negotiating these narratives are generally missing from this discussion, even in my own previous work.

74. Delaney, "Voices," 151.
75. Delaney, "Voices," 151.
76. Delaney, "Voices," 151.
77. Kim, "Gender Construction."
78. Miller-McLemore, *Also a Mother*, 118.

1.4.3 Motherhood and Patriarchy: Migrant as Mother

Along with a discourse of homogeneity, the marriage immigrant's role as mother within a patriarchal system is also central to this discussion on multiculturalism in Korea. Hyunok Lee argues that government regulation of international marriage in Korea and Vietnam "is geared toward verifying whether the marriage is genuine, that is, based on the modern conception of voluntary love between individuals."[79] However, this notion of voluntary "love" marriages is deconstructed to reveal an underlying discourse of nation building and reproduction linked to the narrative of patriarchy in Korea. Lee concludes by arguing that the debate between agency and commodification of intimate relations would be more fruitfully directed to discussions of the imagined roles constructed in the discourse of policies which relate to "nation building and reproducing processes."[80] This is not limited to this context. Feminists have recognized that, "It is women's sexuality and reproductive capacity that is the valued commodity."[81] In this sense, patriarchy is more than just the dominance of women, it is when women are utilized to facilitate the "central social relationship" of paternity within a society.[82] More specifically in relation to Korea, the commodification of the women's reproductive abilities is intensified in the context of the patriarchal Korean family system which emphasizes the reproduction of a male heir in order to continue the lineage to secure ancestral obligations.[83] Speaking of Korean families, Myung-Kim argues that this system, rather than being static, provides "an important cultural and political space" to be negotiated by both mother and daughter-in-law.[84] Research indicates that female marriage migrants are also learning ways to negotiate this space.

Talking about Southeast Asian migrant brides, Hyun Mee Kim argues that women in multicultural families are daily using both material and symbolic resources to "establish their social status and stabilize their living conditions," navigating social and familial relationships in ways which are "diverse, fragmented and individualistic."[85] Exploring the extent to which

79. Lee, "Trafficking in Women?," 1256.
80. Lee, "Trafficking in Women?," 1262.
81. Miller-McLemore, *Also a Mother*, 54.
82. Miller-McLemore, *Also a Mother*, 74.
83. Deuchler cited in Kim, "Changing Relationships," 186.
84. Kim, "Changing Relationships," 179.
85. Kim, "State and Migrant Women," 102.

the Western woman raising her child in the Korean context both incorporates her own traditions and adapts her mothering style to the wider social context offers a unique contribution to the discussion.

1.5 Analysis of Literature Review

This study is positioned within the current literature on multiculturalism and international marriage in Korea. It explores issues of homogeneity and patriarchy as they have been discussed in the context of Korea and the way they have influenced and shaped international marriages, particularly in relation to female immigrant spouses. Embedded in this discussion are issues of assimilation and agency, particularly as they have been explored through feminist approaches. It contributes to this literature by adding discussion of the expatriate motherhood experience of Anglophone women in the context of Korea through a qualitative phenomenological methodology.

Marriage immigrant women in Korea become part of a system with expectations of motherhood which they navigate. As I have argued elsewhere,[86] there is an expectation that these women will be integrated into society by fulfilling their role as mothers by producing offspring. It follows that their experience and understanding of discourses of multiculturalism in Korea is linked to how they experience motherhood as expatriates. Others have argued that "For immigrant wives, reproduction is their gendered path to citizenship as good Korean mothers."[87] Consequently, and again consistent with my arguments elsewhere, notions of femininity and motherhood are an integral part of Korea's developing narrative in relation to marriage immigrants.[88] Given that the primary goal of this multicultural narrative in relation to these marriage immigrants is invested in the production of good "Korean" citizens, what happens when the woman's narrative of multiculturalism is at odds with this goal? If this is true for Anglophone women as well, how do they negotiate this narrative if indeed they desire to? On the contrary, if they do desire to raise a "good Korean citizen" how do they go about that when they aren't one themselves? What obstacles or challenges do they face? What systems are available to them which they utilize to achieve their goals? A phenomenological study of a Western woman's experience of motherhood is best suited to answering

86. Kim, "Gender Construction."
87. Cheng, "Sexual Protection," 1628.
88. Kim, "Gender Construction," 22.

these kinds of questions of how multiculturalism is experienced, interpreted, and negotiated. Firstly, it is important to examine more closely what makes the motherhood of a marriage immigrant potentially threatening within the Korean context.

The unique culture that a female international spouse brings to her marriage can be seen as threatening to some in Korean society. More general studies on multiculturalism have recognized that as a social institution, marriage is the context where a majority of cultural values are shared and transmitted.[89] The generally accepted understanding in Korean society is that "Foreign brides are assumed to be carriers of cultural practices and traditions that are different from Korean culture."[90] The negative implications of this sentiment are reflected in the claims that social integration is hindered by the preservation of a migrant woman's culture and is reflected in government policy.[91] Kim Hyun Mee rightly highlights policies which have seen any measures to preserve a migrant woman's culture and language not only as "undesirable" but as a hindrance to "their integration into Korean society."[92] Hence, the female marriage immigrant's culture can conceivably be understood as a potential threat to the social cohesion of a society with a strongly integrated narrative of homogeneity. Furthermore, the threat to homogeneity that immigrant brides pose is intricately linked to their roles as mothers.

The immigrant's role in raising citizens should not be overlooked. In the context of America, Bonnie Miller-McLemore recognizes the role that mothers play in the child's cultural and language development. She makes the profound statement that "I, as mother, have access to the power of nurture and to the integral process whereby the order of culture and language emerges in the life of a child."[93] This has also been recognized in the case of multicultural families in Europe.

"In the context of cross-cultural families, women play a particularly important role in the reproduction of identity at this often unseen, domestic level, by passing down traditions, songs, foods, and other domestic symbols, shaping the narrative of belonging to the common origin, and helping

---

89. Beckett and Macey, "Race, Gender and Sexuality," 312.

90. Kim, "Naturalizing Korean Ethnicity," 193.

91. Kim, "State and Migrant Women," 106.

92. Kim, "State and Migrant Women," 106.

93. Miller-McLemore, *Also a Mother*, 146.

children grow into an existing social world."[94] But does this need to be so threatening to Korean society?

Some studies indicate that integration and negotiation rather than pure cultural assimilation or separation as defined by traditional acculturation theory does in fact take place when raising a child cross-culturally. One study exploring the mothering styles of North American-born second-generation Korean American mothers and their partners did find that the wider social context more than ethnicity or cultural ideology impacted the parenting styles used.[95] There is also evidence of the cultural negotiation taking place within the context of Southeast Asian women marrying Korean men.

The focus on marriage immigrants and their roles as mothers has also been explored by Korean academics. Jung-mee Hwang wrote about immigrant mothers in Korea, although once again the focus was on Asian women. While acknowledging the growing number of immigrant mothers raising children in Korean households and the implications for multiculturalism in Korea, she also (correctly) points out that the majority of these mothers are from China.[96] Hwang makes two observations which are relevant to the current study. First she notes that policies related to these mothers have generally focused on education and cultural adaptation.[97] Secondly, and of even more significance, she makes the point that mothering by these immigrants will be diverse depending on immigration experiences and family background.[98] Once again this suggests that the experience of Western women marrying and mothering in Korea will be different compared to women from other Asian countries, particularly if they do indeed have different paths to migration into Korea. Furthermore, it again suggests a need to examine not only what meaning this Korean discourse of multiculturalism holds for families with Anglophone mothers, but also their awareness and understandings of policies and whether they perceive any advantages or prejudices in them.

The discussion of foreign grooms with Korean spouses also emphasizes the significance of motherhood to the discourse. Although the trend of foreign grooms appears to have preceded the flood of immigrant brides,

---

94. Isaakyan and Triandafyllidou (2014) in Son, *National Identity*, 636.

95. Kim et al., "Relationship-Directed Parenting."

96. Hwang, "Positioning Migrant Mothers," 141.

97. Hwang, "Positioning Migrant Mothers," 141.

98. Hwang, "Positioning Migrant Mothers," 141.

and male spouses from Western countries outweighed the number of brides until recently, it is the current trend which is provoking the development of a national narrative of multiculturalism. Lee et al. argue that it was only after the 1990s that these "immigrant foreign spouses became a visible population in Korea and, together with the even larger population of immigrant laborers, they have challenged the long-held image of a homogeneous Korean society."[99] This further explains the policy development around multicultural marriages. Given that intercultural marriages are becoming a visible part of the population, the policies are an attempt to reestablish some form of cohesion to the disruption to Korea's narrative of homogeneity caused by the introduction of these cultures.

Although Lee et al. suggest that this growing visible presence is only occurring now because the Korean women married to Western men would often live in the husband's country,[100] issues of maternity and patriarchy can also potentially be seen as an influencing factor. Like Nancy Abelmann and Hyunhee Kim have convincingly argued, "non-Korean women have been assimilable into South Korean families, while non-Korean men have been understood to produce non-Korean households."[101] This is why a Western woman marrying a Korean national is a qualitatively different experience than that of a Western man. The Western man's family is not considered a typically "Korean" family due to patriarchy, whereas the Western woman's family potentially is. Subsequently, the Western woman's child-rearing has a potentially different meaning for Korean multiculturalism.

Sarah Son has published the first focused study on the phenomenon of Anglophone Western women married to Koreans residing in Korea. Son interviewed twenty-five women from a wide range of English-speaking Western countries.[102] In some ways her objectives were similar to the current study. Her stated intentions were firstly to shed light on "the social integration of ethnically non-Asian women from Anglophone (English-speaking) countries, married to Korean men and living in South Korea."[103] She comes to the conclusion that in relation to these factors, these women do differ from the more documented experiences of Southeast Asian

---

99. Lee et al., "International Marriages," 165–66.

100. Lee et al., "International Marriages," 165.

101. Abelmann and Kim, "Failed Attempt," 108.

102. Son, *National Identity*, 637.

103. Son, *National Identity*, 630.

women.[104] She also examines how the woman's exploration of her national identity is related to her, "capacity and willingness . . . to integrate in South Korea."[105]

Although Son primarily focused on the expressions of national identity and how differences in experiences are framed in nationalistic ways,[106] a significant finding also suggests the implications of motherhood for the Anglophone marriage immigrant. Son claims that "for Anglophone wives living in South Korea, the creation of a 'new' family culture is an important security-giving process, to insulate the woman against the foreignness of the culture she lives in, and provide a space of comfort and enjoyment where she feels accepted and valued."[107]

Furthermore, Son's findings also demonstrated how the women were navigating their understanding of Korea's patriarchal norms. She describes how there emerged a "negative construction of the 'typical' male of the host culture as overly 'patriarchal,' 'narrow-minded' and 'old-fashioned,' as opposed to the more tolerable, 'open-minded' husband."[108] In addition, Son found a common thread in the interviews where a number of the women understood themselves as playing a participating role in their husband's "liberation" from these patriarchal norms regardless of whether or not their husbands had already started to move away from these norms prior to their relationship.[109]

Son's work is distinguished from the current study in that she did not limit the sample of participants to those women with children. Even so, her findings suggest the experiential impact that motherhood can have. She found that the respondents who did have children all acknowledged the additional pressures related to culture and raising children.[110] She also noted how this was initially related to tensions particularly in the woman's relationship with her mother-in-law.[111] Through framing and focusing the current study through the lens of the participant's experience of motherhood, the current proposed study will be able to provide greater detailed

---

104. Son, *National Identity*, 633.

105. Son, *National Identity*, 630.

106. Son, *National Identity*, 631.

107. Son, *National Identity*, 648.

108. Son, *National Identity*, 641.

109. Son, *National Identity*, 641.

110. Son, *National Identity*, 642.

111. Son, *National Identity*, 642.

insight into the development of how multicultural narratives are negotiated in these families. Even so, Son's findings have important implications for the current study.

Firstly, differences in cultural background (class, culture, religion, etc.) as well as ethnicity, suggest that Anglophone women with a Western-shaped worldview will have a different experience in the way they exercise their agency to negotiate roles and expectations with their husbands and in-laws. As others have suggested,[112] different dynamics are introduced in the case of Western women marriage immigrants. Son, herself a Caucasian Australian-British scholar married to a Korean man, argues that their perceived socioeconomic status, combined with racial hierarchy and stereotypes do not fit with the narrative of hypergamy found in discussions of Asian immigrant brides.[113] She also indicates that the cultural currency of the English language further distinguishes Anglophone women from other groups of international female marriage migrants in terms of employment opportunities.[114] A study conducted of Filipina domestic workers and Taiwanese employers also supports this argument that English can affect relational power dynamics in the context of the power economies of Asia.[115] Furthermore, the tools and strategies these women utilize to preserve and share cultural traditions with their children while navigating the dominant cultural narratives will conceivably differ.

Secondly, the initial purpose of migration to Korea may not only distinguish women spouses from Western countries from those arriving from marriage introduction services, but it may also have a significant influence on their experience. Although Gavin Jones and Hsiu Shen extend the categories of motivating factors for international marriage to overall global mobility due to "tourism, business travel, international study and student exchanges,"[116] they fail to make the connection between these trends and Western immigrant brides in Korea. Unlike women from the aforementioned research seeking immigration through marriage, women from Western countries may have a different immigration journey involving some of the factors mentioned by Jones and Shen. Marriage may not be the primary factor facilitating their immigration. In contrast to what research

112. Son, *National Identity*; Kim, "Daughters-in-Law of Korea?"

113. Son, *National Identity*, 633.

114. Son, *National Identity*, 633–34.

115. Lan, "More Money."

116. Jones and Shen, "International Marriage," 15.

suggests is the dominant trend for women of Southeast Asian countries, marriage for women from Western countries may follow after initial immigration has occurred through other avenues, subsequently leading to relationships which prolong their sojourn in Korea. This will have a qualitative impact on their experience of marriage and motherhood. These factors are all indicated by the specificity principle of acculturation as it is outlined by Marc Bornstein,[117] which is discussed further in chapter 2 in relation to Anglophone immigrant mothers in Korea.

If the Korean discourse of multiculturalism is going to move beyond a mere rhetorical cover for assimilation to serve the social, cultural, reproductive, and even economical needs of Korean society, the discussion needs to extend beyond arguments of hypergamy and the vulnerability or agency of these female South East Asian marriage immigrants. It needs to examine what multiculturalism means to a diverse body of immigrants and how they negotiate the related advantages and frustrations associated with their given context. Keuntae Kim's argument for the recognition of the diversity within international marriages highlights an important next step needed if a healthy sense of multiculturalism is to emerge in Korea.[118]

The Korea Focus section of the online paper Don-a Ilbo,[119] briefly introduced one American, Karen Kim, whose experience demonstrates the connection between child-rearing and patriarchy for Anglophone marriage immigrants in Korea.[120] The article describes how she had settled in Korea as a result of her husband's obligation to his family's clan. Karen's story demonstrates the patriarchal family responsibilities of the firstborn son, particularly when he is the eldest son of the "Head Family," which still exist in Korean society. Furthermore, the article details how the fact that the couple only had daughters and no son had been an "issue" for the family.[121] This demonstrates how the importance of maintaining the patriarchal lineage is still present in parts of Korean society. It is a clear example of how the role of motherhood and the subsequent responsibilities placed on marriage immigrant women can also be experienced by Western

117. Bornstein, "Specificity Principle."

118. Kim, "Cross-Border Marriages."

119. Min, "Karen Kim's Uncommon Life."

120. This is not the Australian Karen Kim conducting the present study, although the title "Karen Kim's Uncommon Life" could definitely be used for an article describing my life married to my Korean husband.

121. Min, "Karen Kim's Uncommon Life."

women in intercultural marriages with Koreans. The three roles of wife, daughter-in-law, and mother present in the dominant multicultural discourse surrounding marriage immigrant women are intricately related. The way that these women navigate multiculturalism and these roles in Korea is heavily tied to their experience of motherhood and raising their child in a host country.

In addition to Son's findings, this proposed research contributes to the literature by presenting the experiences of Anglophone women negotiating Korean discourses of multiculturalism on a personal level as they raise their multiracial children multiculturally in Korea. It is hoped that this will serve to further break down stereotypes and contribute diversity to the connotation and understanding of a multicultural family in Korean society. Failing to understand and discuss the variety and forms these families represent as well as their unique experiences will only serve to further position them as "other," rather than seeing them truly embraced and integrated as part of the Korean society.

Given the other factors influencing the multicultural narrative of South Korea, such as patriarchy, the chronically low birth rate and the resulting emphasis on an immigrant woman's role as mother, the experience of a multicultural family with a Western mother and a Korean father will be a different and valuable contribution to the discussion of multiculturalism in Korea. The question posed by this research is essentially, "What does it mean for Western, Anglophone women to raise a multiracial child in a society which emphasizes their responsibility to raise 'Good Korean' citizens?" This question is raised with the purpose of assessing the suitability of applying Carrie Doehring's feminist pastoral counseling approaches to support these women and their families, along with contributing to the wider discourse on multiculturalism in Korea generally.[122] Given that the focus is on the experiences of these women, a phenomenological qualitative study is deemed best suited to this research question. Before discussing the methodological approach taken in this study in chapter 3, the next chapter will overview feminist and intercultural pastoral care as well as the acculturation theory which lay the foundation for the proposed pastoral approach outlined in chapter 7.

122. Doehring, "Developing Models."

Chapter 2

THEORETICAL BACKGROUND

THE THEORETICAL AND THEOLOGICAL application to this study of the experiences of Anglophone expatriate women raising their biracial children in Korea has been developed from feminist theology and approaches to pastoral care. In this book, feminist pastoral care methods are being considered in light of acculturation theory. The women in the study are dealing with issues of acculturation due to their immigration and international marriage status. Furthermore, this book argues that their acculturation process can be understood as influenced by their status as Western Anglophone women and the unique context of patriarchy and homogeneity that Korea provides as a destination society, which was outlined in chapter 1. Understanding the dynamic nature of the expatriate mother's experience in raising their multicultural child in a host country is an important aspect of providing appropriate pastoral care.

2.1 Feminism, Theology and Pastoral Care

A feminist framework is suited to helping Western women in the Korean context evaluate, understand, and negotiate the ideologies, discourses, and social structures which they encounter in their acculturation process. Feminists have been described as having three primary concerns, "femaleness (a matter of biology), femininity, ("a set of culturally defined characteristics"), and feminism ("the struggle against patriarchy and sexism").[1] These concerns are all reflected in feminist pastoral theologian Bonnie Miller-McLemore's articulation of a feminist perspective which she argues, "demands a critical analysis of structures and ideologies that rank people as inferior or superior according to various traits of human nature, whether gender, sexual orientation, class, color, age, physical ability, and so forth."[2] She describes four practices of *compassionate resistance, empowerment, nurturance,* and *liberation* which she sees as central to this approach.[3] These practices entail the associated tasks of confrontation and advocacy in the face of violence and abuse as well as empowering others to do the same.[4] In her earlier work, Carrie Doehring argues that feminist pastoral counseling should primarily seek to liberate and empower.[5] She understands liberation as "not simply *liberation from* the ways we have been constricted and oppressed within and without by patriarchal structures, but *liberation into* the fullness of being we know through glimpses of our true selves and God."[6]

Writing in 1992, Doehring claimed that she was only at that time beginning to see discussions of pastoral counseling from a feminist perspective especially when addressing sexual abuse and violence.[7] These feminist concerns are now notably reflected in the work of Pamela Cooper-White, Kirsten Leslie, and Marie M. Fortune, all of which examine pastoral and theological approaches to violence and issues of abuse against women, including that which occurs in intimate relationships.[8]

As well as exploring issues of physical and systematic violence, a pastoral theology influenced by feminism has highlighted concerns related to inclusion, identity, and mutual influence. In *Theories of Culture,* feminist theologian Kathryn Tanner deconstructs the notion of a Christian identity. After providing a very valuable history and background as to the way we currently understand the word culture, particularly in the Western anthropological sense, Tanner builds on this foundation to search for how

---

1. Moi cited in Doehring, "Developing Models," 101.

2. Miller-McLemore, "Feminist Theory," 79.

3. Miller-McLemore, "Feminist Theory," 80.

4. Miller-McLemore, "Feminist Theory," 80.

5. Doehring, "Developing Models," 23.

6. Doehring, "Developing Models," 25–26.

7. Doehring, "Developing Models," 23.

8. Cooper-White, *The Cry of Tamar*; Leslie, *Violence is No Stranger*; Fortune, *Sexual Violence.*

to define and understand a Christian identity. Significantly, she argues that boundaries between Christian and nonChristian ways of life are fluid and a process of mutual influence. She also argues that "Christian identity is therefore no longer a matter of unmixed purity, but a hybrid affair established through unusual uses of materials."[9] This approach, replacing the notion of boundaries, while recognizing differences exist, in favor of a concept of "mutual influence" is a useful alternative to narratives of boundaries or borders. It also proposes how outside cultural materials are used and incorporated into a sense of self at the boundaries where mutual influence occurs. Although useful in creating an understanding of a more inclusive Christian identity, other feminist theological approaches are more directly related to the issues which are the focus of this current study.

Issues related to inequalities caused by the devaluation of domestic duties especially in relation to child-rearing are challenged by social feminists in particular.[10] As seen in the previous chapter, the focus on the female immigrant's role of mother as it relates to the patriarchal goal of maintaining paternal lineage is exasperated by the declining birth rate and complicated by a discourse of homogeneity in Korea. This is important context for international marriages between an Anglophone woman and a Korean man, particularly when discussing her role as a mother. Miller-McLemore argues that concerns over social inequalities, including how they relate to domestic duties, aptly position a social feminist approach to address pastoral theology which she sees as working "at the intersection of personal experience, tradition, culture, and community."[11]

Miller-McLemore also sees other approaches to feminist theory influencing feminist pastoral theology. Gynocentric feminists emphasize how relational forms of knowledge and the female body have been denied leading to oppression in patriarchal systems.[12] This approach has been identified in the work of feminist pastoral theologians focusing on "women centered knowledge" alongside concerns for rights and equality.[13] Although not solely definitive of her approach, the influence of gynocentric feminism in terms of valuing forms of knowledge connected to the woman's body are somewhat reflected in Miller-McLemore's own work.

---

9. Tanner, *Theories of Culture*, 152.

10. Miller-McLemore, "Feminist Theory," 82.

11. Miller-McLemore, "Feminist Theory," 82.

12. Miller-McLemore, "Feminist Theory," 83.

13. Miller-McLemore, "Feminist Theory," 89.

2.1.1 Bonnie Miller-McLemore's Theology of Motherhood

In her book *Also a Mother*, Bonnie Miller-McLemore seeks to develop a maternal theology based on the negotiation of valid female vocations and generative concerns of motherhood and work outside the home while giving appropriate significance to each.[14] In doing so, she devotes a chapter to discussing how the physical experience of motherhood including birth and lactation give way to particular bodily forms of knowledge. Her approach outlined in *Also a Mother* has been described as taking a combined hermeneutical and emancipatory praxis method.[15] Hermeneutical methods are seen as those which rely "heavily on philosophical sources and norms in addition to social scientific and theological sources and norms."[16] An emancipatory praxis views understanding and interpretation as part of a broader process of emancipation and social justice.[17]

Miller-McLemore argues that mothers are often caught between values represented by the two vocations of motherhood and work outside the home. She claims, "Many people are not so much *without* a culture as caught *between* cultures that have widely divergent, frequently clashing, strikingly compelling standards."[18] She also sees community as crucial to empowering mothers to navigate the cultural clashes she describes. She challenges the discourse of unconditional maternal sacrifice, arguing that "Mutual regard and self-giving belong within a more comprehensive context of familial, social, and cultural support. Mutual love is the ideal. But particularly with children, mutual love does not begin mutually."[19] In other words, she is arguing that a supportive community is needed in order to offset the emotional and physical demands of raising a child, particularly early on.

2.1.1.1 Theological Reflections on the Narrative of Ruth

In seeking understanding of the cultural clashes facing women in their search for generativity, Miller-McLemore turns to the narrative of Ruth

14. Miller-McLemore, *Also a Mother*.

15. Doehring, "Feminist Pastoral Theology," 105.

16. Doehring, "Feminist Pastoral Theology," 105.

17. Doehring, "Feminist Pastoral Theology," 105.

18. Miller-McLemore, *Also a Mother*, 30.

19. Miller-McLemore, *Also a Mother*, 166.

located in the Old Testament of the Bible for theological reflection. She notes how this Hebrew narrative of Ruth and Naomi "for centuries has provided a compelling image of women caught between cultures."[20] As a first step in developing her theology of motherhood Miller-McLemore argues for a rereading of the narrative which she labels "Revisiting Orpah."[21] For her, this involves a more critical reading of Ruth and Naomi as "faultless exemplars of selflessness and devotion" and a "more generous" reading of Orpah.[22] She further argues that all three of the women in the opening chapter of the narrative "function as realistic examples of complicated responses to cultural upheaval."[23]

Miller-McLemore sees the two mother's houses in the book of Ruth symbolically as the two cultures a modern woman must navigate, with traditional maternal roles represented by Orpah's choice and Naomi representing feminist theology.[24] She also highlights their use of "moral and religious agency" in the aftermath of the death of the males in their family, but also the narrative's "strikingly unconventional" use of the *mother's* house.[25] Citing Phyllis Trible who understands Ruth and Naomi as "women in culture, women against culture, and women transforming culture," Miller-McLemore argues that "Orpah represents the woman caught between cultures"[26] in the sense of her making the unconventional choice of her mother's house in a patriarchal society. She further claims that Naomi's petition to her daughters-in-law to return to their mother's house "protests a system in which men control motherhood in order to maintain patriarchy."[27] This echoes previous assertions on the current discourse on international marriages in Korea. Miller-McLemore sees the overarching application of the narrative in terms of how "People today are a caught in a struggle to redefine 'family,' 'people,' 'God,' and 'home' in a foreign land."[28] For the marriage immigrant raising her child in Korea, however, this struggle is far more literal. This connection between the narrative of Ruth

20. Miller-McLemore, *Also a Mother*, 86.

21. Miller-McLemore, *Also a Mother*, 177–79.

22. Miller-McLemore, *Also a Mother*, 177.

23. Miller-McLemore, *Also a Mother*, 177.

24. Miller-McLemore, *Also a Mother*, 180.

25. Miller-McLemore, *Also a Mother*, 178.

26. Miller-McLemore, *Also a Mother*, 177.

27. Miller-McLemore, *Also a Mother*, 178.

28. Miller-McLemore, *Also a Mother*, 180.

and immigration has however been made by others who have conducted theological reflections on the book of Ruth in relation to both the Korean and the American immigration context.

2.1.1.1.1 THE NARRATIVE OF RUTH: THEOLOGICAL REFLECTIONS ON IMMIGRATION

M. Daniel Carroll R. and Yeong-mee Lee have both theologically examined female migration utilizing the Ruth narrative.[29] Lee draws parallels between the biblical narrative of Ruth as a marriage migrant and South East Asian marriage immigrants in Korea from a feminist theological perspective. She has three premises for her comparisons. Firstly, she claims that in both cases the reason and form of migration are poverty and intermarriage.[30] Furthermore, she claims that the migration occurred in societies where they experienced "cultural discrimination and segregation from the natives" and where their lives as migrants can be depicted as a "struggle of survival."[31] Others would argue that this emphasis on economic factors as a primary motivation for marriage migration is an oversimplification.[32] Other feminist work on the phenomenon focuses more on the proactive agency of the women migrants as active agents in the immigration process. This is seen particularly in Caren Freeman and Hyunjoo Jung's work.[33] In addition, while examining the book of Ruth from the perspective of immigration and assimilation in the context of America, M. Daniel Carroll R. views Ruth as a much more proactive agent than does Lee.

Drawing on his guatemalidad identity, Carroll applies the story of Ruth to the immigrant experience of his family. He concludes his observations by arguing that Ruth overcame obstacles which are similar to those facing contemporary immigrants in America.[34] He emphasizes the process reflected in Ruth's "hard work and loyalty, coupled with creative (even risky

---

29. M. Daniel Carroll R. from the American context ("Once a Stranger") and Yeong-mee Lee from the Korean context ("Ruth and Marriage").

30. Lee, "Ruth and Marriage," 117.

31. Lee, "Ruth and Marriage," 117.

32. Particularly Kim, "Daughters-in-Law of Korea?" 3.

33. Freeman, *Making and Faking Kinship*; "Marrying Up." Also, Jung, "Let Their Voices."

34. Carroll R., "Once a Stranger," 188.

action)" in facing challenges of "physical and economic survival, ethnic acceptance, cultural competence and legal awareness."[35]

Carroll's reading of Ruth is one with empowering application for immigrants. This is most evident in his referencing Ruth's place in the lineage of Jesus, alongside the observation that immigrant parents, as evidenced by Ruth, could potentially be part of a "significant trajectory" even if they themselves do not necessarily see the completion of the process.[36] He concludes his paper with a profound statement rich with application for the current study.

> For people who are the product of ethnic intermarriage—in my case, the son of an immigrant mother and a native-born father—we have heard the stories of that parent who worked so hard for us to feel at home here while not losing our other cultural identity (for me, my guatemalidad). We are Obed. Said another way: Ruth still lives among us.[37]

There is broad scope for application here and potential for not only the biracial child such as Carroll, but also the immigrant mother, to find herself in the narrative.

In addition to Carroll's reading, the implication of motherhood and immigration can be understood in other ways through the Ruth narrative. The genealogy of Jesus given in the book of Matthew reveals that Boaz, the kinsman redeemer who Ruth eventually marries, was also the son of a multicultural marriage. The Gospel of Matthew adds to the narrative of Rahab, the prostitute from Jericho whose interactions with the Israelites are outlined in Joshua, revealing that after Jericho fell, she married an Israelite man and gave birth to Boaz (Matthew 1:5; Joshua 2; NIV). What does it say of her acceptance into the Israelite community that this former prostitute would raise a son who was described in the book of Ruth as such an upstanding Israelite citizen,[38] who adhered to the law of Yahweh during the time of the judges where there is the widely repeated lament that "everyone did as he saw fit"?[39] What does it say about Boaz's integration into the society that he was considered to be such an upright and law-abiding Israelite that his multicultural heritage from a Gentile prostitute was not

35. Carroll R., "Once a Stranger," 188.

36. Carroll R., "Once a Stranger," 188.

37. Carroll R., "Once a Stranger," 188.

38. Trible, *God and the Rhetoric*, 175–76; Webb, *Five Festival Garments*, 44.

39. Zondervan, *NIV Study Bible*, 327, 365.

even thought significant enough to mention? Had he become so integrated that his multicultural heritage had been forgotten? Had his mother been lost to a patriarchal system? Surely the book of Ruth has pastoral counseling applications for the expatriate mother, but also for the community which embraces them.

In his links between immigration and the narrative of Ruth, Carroll also recognizes that the extent of assimilation is left vague. He draws on an assimilation reading of the book of Ruth noting that while historical context may differ, similarities can potentially be drawn based on shared human experience.[40] He describes how "Ruth assimilates *to some degree* into Israelite culture"[41] suggesting that she must have become somewhat proficient in the Hebrew language to communicate with her Israelite in-laws.[42] Elsewhere he notes that ambiguities in her assimilation are to be expected due to the nuanced balancing of personal motives to achieve success and survival when facing obstacles in a host country.[43] He elaborates that despite her pledge in the opening chapter which is worded as a strong proclamation of faith and loyalty to both Naomi and her God, nowhere does she use the name of the God of Israel, again calling into question the nature of her assimilation.[44] He recognizes that questions of whether or not Ruth's assimilation was motivated by faith or a desire for acceptance and survival alongside questions of how much of her Moabite culture was retained are not addressed by the text. But even how he sees these questions as being raised by the text demonstrates the parallels it shares with the participants in the current study. The fact that these questions of acculturation can be raised from the narrative, also further supports a reading of acculturation which is personalized to the woman experiencing the immigration, rather than a rigid model which discounts individual experience.

Carroll's reflections also highlight the importance of community in the immigration process. He describes Ruth as utilizing three primary social networks to facilitate assimilation.[45] Significantly, he highlights not only "the family of Naomi" (Ruth's in-laws), but also her decision to "remain in

---

40. Carroll R., "Once a Stranger," 185.
41. Italics added for emphasis.
42. Carroll, *Christians at the Border*, 75.
43. Carroll R., "Once a Stranger," 185.
44. Carroll R., "Once a Stranger," 187.
45. Carroll R., "Once a Stranger," 186.

this network."[46] Furthermore, he sees noteworthy how these communities refer to Ruth without the use of her name. "She is the 'Moabitess' (2:6), 'the woman' (4:11), 'this young woman' (4:12), and 'your daughter-in-law' (4:15). In other words, Ruth is *among* them and appreciated *by* them, but still not *of* them."[47] These themes identified by Carroll reflect aspects of acculturation theory which can be combined with Carrie's Doehring's practice of pastoral care to approach the phenomenon of Anglophone expatriate motherhood in the context of Korea.

2.1.2 Carrie Doehring's Practice of Pastoral Care

In her book, *The Practice of Pastoral Care*,[48] Doehring outlines a postmodern critical correlational method. This method is a cross-disciplinary dialogical approach which seeks to incorporate sources from different disciplines together.[49] She describes her approach as trifocal where she highlights the role of *premodern*, *modern*, and *postmodern* lenses through which to apply pastoral care.[50] She describes one of the uses of the *premodern* lens as drawing on sacred texts as well as religious experiences or practices.[51] Furthermore, the *modern* lens can be applied through the use of biblical criticism as well as other methods. The *postmodern lens* understands knowledge as provisional and contextual.[52] For Doehring the use of a critical correlational method postmodernly "is not to generate universal knowledge and theories, but to develop contextual understandings of persons in crisis and formulate strategies for seeking their wellbeing and justice."[53]

The approach outlined by Doehring occurs in a number of stages. It begins with the careseeker's approach to care by recognizing the need for empathy, awareness of power dynamics, and reflection on how the careseeker's own experiences contribute to the development of the caregiving

---

46. Carroll R., "Once a Stranger," 186.

47. Carroll R., "Once a Stranger," 186.

48. Doehring, *Pastoral Care.*

49. Poling and Miller (1985); Browning (1991); Doehring (1999); Ramsay (1998). Cited in Doehring, *Pastoral Care,* 9.

50. Doehring, *Pastoral Care,* 2.

51. Doehring, *Pastoral Care,* 2.

52. Doehring, *Pastoral Care,* 2.

53. Doehring, *Pastoral Care,* 9.

relationship. After developing the caregiving relationship, she discusses a psychological assessment of the careseeker which reflects on loss, violence, and compulsive behaviors.[54] Following a psychological assessment, the plan of care turns to an assessment of the careseeker's relational and cultural networks and systems.

For Doehring the purpose of the assessment of family, community, and culture is in determining their contribution in the construction of "stories that can imprison or liberate."[55] As part of this assessment, she proposes two questions: "In what ways do these relational systems help the careseeker mourn her losses, survive violence, and cope with stress? Do any of them intensify her suffering?"[56]

In the final step before developing a plan of care, Doehring describes theological reflection which she argues is a "way to talk about people's deepest values."[57] She distinguishes between *embedded theology* which consists of the deeply embedded beliefs which shape the careseeker's worldviews and practices, and *deliberative theology,* which is the person's more formally processed and articulated beliefs.[58] The contribution of this step is in being able to identify theological perspectives which are contextually significant, enable engagement with other disciplines, and provide a pragmatic foundation for providing care and justice.[59]

After the psychological and cultural assessments and theological reflection, a plan of care is prepared which Doehring further outlines as occurring in three stages. These are: "(1) attending to the careseeker's safety and building trust, (2) mourning losses, and (3) reconnecting with life."[60] She proposes that this approach can be used in crisis care when addressing themes of "loss, violence, and compulsive ways of coping."[61] Doehring herself claims her approach focuses on crisis intervention in terms of loss or the experience of violence which is specific to her North American context.[62] Her understanding of loss includes seasons of transitions of which

54. Doehring, *Pastoral Care*, 65–85.

55. Doehring, *Pastoral Care*, 69.

56. Doehring, *Pastoral Care*, 97.

57. Doehring, *Pastoral Care*, 111.

58. Doehring, *Pastoral Care*, 112.

59. Doehring, *Pastoral Care*, 12.

60. Doehring, *Pastoral Care*, 133.

61. Doehring, *Pastoral Care*, 133.

62. Doehring, *Pastoral Care*, 7.

she specifically identifies becoming a parent and even entering or ending a committed relationship.[63] There are aspects of Doehring's method which are a useful foundation for approaching the particular international marriage phenomenon being outlined in this study as well as those which need further consideration.

Doehring's approach is potentially useful for the current situation under study in the sense that it incorporates a systematic assessment of the careseeker's culture, communities, and family, and even extends to advocacy through social systems and can include a social identity assessment. The point where Doehring's theory most closely addresses the issues which this book argues needs specific attention is in relation to cultural systems. She claims that in order to examine how cultural systems are impacting the crisis, a caregiver first needs to explore how "the careseeker's narrative and identity are shaped by her culture, that is, the practices that transmit a culture's knowledge, beliefs, morals, law, and customs."[64] Furthermore, she herself describes how her "approach to pastoral care begins with pastoral care conversations and *careseeker's narratives about self, family, community, and culture.*"[65]

Like Doehring, what is being proposed is the need to start with the careseeker's narratives describing their own understanding of their experience. Particularly in situations where a woman has yet to articulate how her understanding of her experience of motherhood has been influenced by the culture and society she resides in and has married into, the very process of exploring these themes may be therapeutic and empowering in and of itself. Doehring correctly argues that a person's life is "inextricably interwoven with the lives of a partner and/or close friends, her family, and those with whom she lives, works, and worships" with subsequent implications for their psychological, physical, and spiritual wellbeing.[66] She further argues how these factors contribute to the formation of an individual's narrative of how they understand their experiences in ways which have the potential to be both transformational and limiting.[67] This influence is reciprocal from a systems perspective which views relational embeddedness as mutually transformational as "change to individuals inevitably involves change

---

63. Doehring, *Pastoral Care*, 11.
64. Doehring, *Pastoral Care*, 100.
65. Doehring, *Pastoral Care*, 166. Italics added for emphasis.
66. Doehring, *Pastoral Care*, 97.
67. Doehring, *Pastoral Care*, 97.

within that person's relational network."[68] Subsequently, it is difficult to assess the pastoral care needs of an expatriate mother until understanding of her personal experience of immigration, marriage, and motherhood is gained, especially in regards to how she has personally weaved together the different cultures into her personal and family narratives and values.

Both Miller-McLemore and Doehring identify the importance of community and society in terms of their pastoral care approach. As mentioned previously, Miller-McLemore sees the need for the support of a community in order for a woman to navigate her dual generative vocations of motherhood and careers outside the house.[69] For Doehring, this takes the form of assessing the careseeker's closest relationships in terms of how these relationships either intensify or help them "mourn her losses, survive her violence, and cope with stress."[70] Indeed the significance and need of community is even indicated in the previously cited study conducted with marriage migrants located in Busan. This study found that "The mental health of marriage migrants is related to their social support networks or relationships, which contribute to reducing acculturation stress and depression."[71] An effective pastoral care approach to expatriate mothers will consider what these communities look like for her, what forms they take, how they are utilized and how the mother is locating, identifying, and utilizing support and community.

2.1.3 Limitations to Miller-McLemore and Doehring

Although a feminist pastoral theology approach offers a promising model for the care of Anglophone expatriate mothers, there are contextual limitations. In her assessment of the relationship between feminist theory and feminist pastoral care, Miller-McLemore not only acknowledges the limits of "one's vantage point" or perspective to the development of the new definitions of pastoral care, but also how these discussions have been heavily influenced by European American Protestants.[72] In terms of her theology of motherhood, the American context is the foundation to her discussion of the conflicts women who wish to seek dual vocations face, which cannot

---

68. Doehring, *Pastoral Care*, 140.

69. Miller-McLemore, *Also a Mother*.

70. Doehring, *Pastoral Care*, 97.

71. Im et al., "Acculturation Stress," 502.

72. Miller-McLemore, "Feminist Theory," 89.

account for the additional stress of understanding the nuances of a host society and the associated expectations. Acknowledging these limitations, she herself invites other voices and viewpoints into the discussion in her preface to that text[73] and again in later works.[74]

The influence of the American context to Doehring's work is also seen in her understanding of liberation as "*liberation into* the fullness of being we know through glimpses of our true selves and God."[75] Embedded within this understanding of liberation are Western values which David Augsburger identifies in Western approaches to measuring mental health in terms of "self-reliance, self-sufficiency, and inner-directed responsibilities for oneself and an internal sense of personal identity."[76] Adding caution to the uncritical use of self-actualization as a goal of pastoral care in the context of Korea are studies which have shown that among ethnically Asian female immigrant spouses, the retention of cultural collectivism contributed to their overall life satisfaction in Korea.[77]

It would be incorrect however to say that Doehring is unaware of the risks of focusing solely on the individual in care. She argues that the emphasis placed on the care of individuals in individualistic cultures reduces the caregiver's understanding of context which she states gives important insight into how cultural context has formed the individual and also limits the carer's ability to understand how social privilege or disadvantage has contributed to the crisis.[78] In the case of expatriate mothers where a woman is removed from the context which helped shaped her, and becomes confronted with her embedded beliefs and values through the experience of motherhood, context gains an additional layer.

Marriage immigrants who become mothers in their destination country experience the transitions which come with marriage, pregnancy, and childbirth, which Doehring describes. In addition, however, the experience of relocating and adjusting to life in a new host country comes with specific gains, losses, and needs which Doehring does not specifically address. It possibly could be argued that this can be dealt with in her generic cultural assessment, however, the experience of expatriate parenting and socializing

---

73. Miller-McLemore, *Also a Mother*, 15.

74. Miller-McLemore, "Feminist Theory," 89.

75. Doehring, "Developing Models," 26.

76. Augsburger, "Pastoral Counselling," 319.

77. Oh et al., "Asian Cultural Collectivism," 24.

78. Doehring, *Pastoral Care*, 166.

a child in a foreign culture has the potential to be so transformative that it needs specific attention. Becoming a parent in a destination country with a spouse from that country is both a significant and specific enough experience that it warrants elaboration. The acculturation process plays an important part in understanding the narrative of their personal experience, the cultural values they hold for themselves and their family, and their status in their country of destination. All of this may provoke needs which are more nuanced than the crisis intervention care Doehring describes, while not ignoring the fact that at times crisis intervention may necessarily be the focus. Essentially context plays a role beyond status and the presence or lack of privilege which contributes to a crisis. The process of mutual influence in terms of value systems needs to be taken into careful consideration when considering Anglophone mothers in the context of Korea. This is where feminist pastoral theories can be enhanced through perspectives from David Augsburger's theories on pastoral counseling across cultures and acculturation theory.

2.2 Feminist Pastoral Care and Pastoral Counseling Across Cultures

David Augsburger's *Pastoral Counseling Across Cultures* provides a broad framework which contributes to effective pastoral care in instances where the counseling relationship consists of people from different cultures. He intentionally chooses the term intercultural as opposed to multicultural or a number of other alternatives in order to emphasize a state of cultural awareness.[79] "Awareness of one's own culture can free one to disconnect identity from cultural externals and to live on the boundary, crossing over and coming back with increasing freedom."[80] Even if externally a care provider appears to share the same culture as the Anglophone expatriate mother in Korea, her marriage to a Korean places both her and the counselor at this boundary that Augsburger describes.

Pastoral Counseling Across Cultures begins with a description of the need for pastoral counselors to have an appreciation, firstly, for the ways in which all individuals, including themselves, have been developmentally influenced by their social and cultural context in addition to the "validity" of

---

79. Augsburger, *Pastoral Counseling*, 13.

80. Augsburger, *Pastoral Counseling*, 13.

other cultural perspectives.[81] This description transitions to explorations of culture, individuality, controls, values, family systems, sexual roles, ethics, possession, psychopathology, and models of psychotherapy."[82]

A definition of values is important to this understanding of intercultural care. According to Augsburger, "Values are the core motivations of the human person" as well as "the broad principles (guides to behaviour) assumed by each culture, transmitted from generation to generation, and operative in the daily life of its members."[83] He identifies certain universal values while acknowledging the potential for them to be expressed slightly differently across cultures.[84] He lists these as the need for preservation and continuation of society, safety, and security and "respect for and conformity within social relationships with fellow human beings."[85] Alongside universal values, Augsburger distinguishes and describes values held by different societies which are also implied in his definition.

Particularly relevant to the current study is Augsburger's distinction between the values of Western and more traditional societies. Western ideals, particularly as they are expressed in America, are described as "unlimited self-reliance and unlimited equality."[86] These are the values which these societies strive towards as a whole regardless of the level to which they are actually realized in practice.[87] They also translate into Western understandings of the purpose of the family and society. "The function of the family of origin is to launch the developing individual; of the family of marriage to provide individual need fulfilment without limiting the autonomy of the person; of the community to provide a secure, open social context for individual achievements and self-realization."[88] This is contrasted with hierarchical structuring of respect and obedience which are held as central in what Augsburger labels more "traditional societies."[89]

81. Augsburger, *Pastoral Counseling*, 14.

82. Augsburger, *Pastoral Counseling*, 14.

83. Augsburger, *Pastoral Counseling*, 145.

84. Augsburger, *Pastoral Counseling*, 149.

85. Augsburger, *Pastoral Counseling*, 149.

86. Augsburger, *Pastoral Counseling*, 155.

87. Augsburger, *Pastoral Counseling*, 155.

88. Augsburger, *Pastoral Counseling*, 364.

89. Augsburger, *Pastoral Counseling*, 164.

Augsburger outlines filial piety as one example of a hierarchal value system held by many traditional societies.[90] Filial piety, which is common in Asian societies including Korea, is where relationships carry a hierarchy of responsibility and obligation.[91] Under this hierarchical value system the primary obligation is towards one's parents, followed by "sibling, sovereign, spouse and friend."[92] This sense of obligation can have implications for decision-making and the choices which are made given that it carries with it a demand for absolute obedience in the classic system.[93] It isn't difficult to imagine how these competing values could at times confront international couples with challenging decisions as to how to honor both value systems. Furthermore, it is possible to see how an unmitigated feminist approach without sensitivity to the particular consequences of systematic and hierarchical responsibilities and even one's desire to adhere to them, could also be problematic.

Augsburger recognizes the conflict presented by the ethical dilemmas which arise "at the boundary of self-realization vs. communal obligation and the contrast of vertical obligations to preceding generations vs. horizontal commitments."[94] He also sees the impact that these values have in differences between Western women and Asian women and their respective objectives and goals.[95] He claims that women from the non-Western world, in which he includes Asia specifically, have "immediate and specific goals" which are more related to "family economics and less on individual advancement or sexually defined liberation."[96] At the same time it is important not to assume the ways in which an individual navigates this boundary nor their level of comfort in doing so. A woman who has been exposed to contrasting values through immigration, especially immigration through marriage, may have altered her priorities. Subsequently, there needs to be a way to measure and account for this process, a task for which acculturation theory offers a promising solution. Firstly, however, an approach which allows the caregiver to listen sensitively to this process is necessary.

90. Augsburger, *Pastoral Counseling*, 164.
91. Augsburger, *Pastoral Counseling*, 164.
92. Augsburger, *Pastoral Counseling*, 164.
93. Augsburger, *Pastoral Counseling*, 165.
94. Augsburger, *Pastoral Counseling*, 261.
95. Augsburger, *Pastoral Counseling*, 227.
96. Augsburger, *Pastoral Counseling*, 227.

In order for a pastoral counselor or carer to accurately assess the systems of a marriage immigrant mother seeking care, they firstly need to have an awareness of how their backgrounds have contributed to their acculturation decisions. Furthermore, it is important to recognize the validity of the mother's cultural affiliations and expressions whilst being sensitive to the fact that these may or may not be what is expected. Augsburger's theory of interpathy provides a better model for achieving this than Doehring's empathy which she lists in her approach as one aspect of the carer-careseeker relationship. This is especially true when empathy is understood as assuming a common cultural base as Augsburger claims.[97]

2.2.1 Empathy versus Interpathy

Augsburger contrasts empathy with the interpathy required of an intercultural counselor. Doehring understands empathy as:

> a means of imaginatively stepping into the shoes of another person
> and seeing the world from her or his perspective. However, at the
> same time they make this connection, caregivers must maintain
> their own perspective and be aware of what is happening within
> both themselves and the caring relationship.[98]

Augsburger provides a very similar definition to empathy as Doehring, however, he emphasizes that the kind of imagining of the experience of another described in empathy is limited to "the context of the individual."[99] In other words, he argues that the imagining that empathy requires can only extend as far as the cultural context is shared.

Augsburger contrasts empathy with interpathy where one intentionally brackets their own beliefs and values in order to comprehend and affectively experience feelings and thoughts emerging from a different frame of assumptions.[100] "In interpathic caring, I, the culturally different, seek to learn and fully entertain within my consciousness a foreign belief."[101] The interpathy Augsburger describes requires a posture of learning from the careseeker about their experience, valuing these experiences as unique to

---

97. Augsburger, *Pastoral Counseling*, 20.

98. Doehring, *Pastoral Care*, 18.

99. Augsburger, *Pastoral Counseling*, 28.

100. Augsburger, *Pastoral Counseling*, 29.

101. Augsburger, *Pastoral Counseling*, 30.

them and a sensitivity to any assumptions that the caregiver brings to their understanding of these experiences as it is described by the careseeker.[102] This posture provides a better foundation to understanding the acculturation experience of expatriate mothers as it is expressed through her narratives of family. Indeed, Augsburger also makes this connection to some extent.[103]

Augsburger describes people in intercultural or multicultural relationships and marriages as bicultural and understands interpathy as a crucial skill for their treatment.[104] Bicultural according to Augsburger refers to "persons who live in a third culture that develops between or on the boundary of two or more adjacent cultures."[105] He acknowledges the potential for bicultural people to be equally comfortable in both cultures but also recognizes the potential for internal or relational tension to develop.[106] Consequently, he argues that "the development of interpathic cross-cultural insight and awareness is highly necessary to work on this boundary, to consult with and refer to therapists within the adjacent cultures and to assist clients."[107]

Interpathy as defined by Augsburger also has implications for the development of a care plan. Through interpathy, a carer must be able to see beyond their own cultural preferences for how people are controlled by either internalizing societal norms in contrast to an external control in relation to their community, as well as assumptions about the way this orientation relates to the individual's context.[108] "Mental health is not defined by either end of the continuum but by the appropriate balance within the person and congruence with the cultural context."[109] In this sense an interpathic counselor will not only be able to respect the integrity of a particular set of values an individual holds, however different they may be from their own, but be sensitive in their understanding of how the individual's context is challenging these values in order to help them to navigate an appropriate response which honors both the individual and the context. That being

102. Augsburger, *Pastoral Counseling*, 29–30.
103. Augsburger, *Pastoral Counseling*, 363.
104. Augsburger, *Pastoral Counseling*, 363.
105. Augsburger, *Pastoral Counseling*, 363.
106. Augsburger, *Pastoral Counseling*, 363.
107. Augsburger, *Pastoral Counseling*, 363.
108. Augsburger, *Pastoral Counseling*, 93.
109. Augsburger, *Pastoral Counseling*, 93.

said, it is also necessary to have a framework from which to understand the way in which these values are being modified and adjusted in relation to other values, particularly within the individual. Acculturation theory provides this framework.

2.3 Acculturation Theory

As discussed in the previous chapter, the international marriage trend in Korea has been approached academically in a variety of ways including discussions on issues of the acculturation and mental health of Asian immigrant brides.[110] In these studies acculturation has been used either loosely or in a strictly technical sense with a slight difference in the emphasis on either the individual or the mutual influence which takes place in the exchange with the community. For example, in the study of the life satisfaction of Asian immigrant brides in Korea, acculturation was used to refer "primarily to immigrants' adoption of the cultural values, traditions, and standards of the host society."[111] This definition focuses on the individual immigrant. A broader definition suggesting mutual influence has been used by Hyun-Sil Kim.[112] Kim drew on the premise that the interaction of "values, beliefs, habits, practices and preferences in lifestyle" which occurs in immigration can potentially impact both the immigrant and the destination society in ways which result in the creation of "a new cultural ecology that is not necessarily consistent with that of either the native or the new society."[113] Both of these usages reflect aspects of a broader acculturation theory.

Although acculturation has been used with different focuses in terms of the impact it has on both society and the individual, John Berry has been recognized as an established leader in acculturation theory internationally.[114] His theories provide the platform from which he and other scholars

---

110. Chung and Lim, "Marriage Immigrant"; Won and Kim, "Family Values; Kim, et al., "Fair Treatment"; Im et al., "Acculturation Stress"; Oh et al., "Asian Cultural Collectivism"; Kim, "Social Integration."

111. Oh et al., "Asian Cultural Collectivism," 26.

112. Kim, "Social Integration."

113. Abraido-Lanza, Ambrister, Florez, and Aguirre cited in Kim, "Social Integration," 562.

114. Ward and Kus, "Back To and Beyond," 472.

are still discussing and building on the term.[115] Berry defines acculturation as "the dual process of cultural and psychological change that takes place as a result of contact between two or more cultural groups and their individual members.[116] Berry's understanding of this process is multifaceted in many ways.

> There are large group and individual differences in how people (in both groups in contact) go about their acculturation (described in terms of the integration, assimilation, separation and marginalization strategies), in how much stress they experience, and how well they adapt psychologically and socioculturally.[117]

The following section elaborates on these dimensions of his acculturation theory.

In 1980 Berry defined four main acculturation strategies ethnocultural groups lean towards when confronted with alternative cultures.[118] Although these categories developed over time, they came to be known as assimilation, integration, separation, and marginalization, all of which describe variations in the extent to which an individual is orientated toward their destination culture and their culture of origin.[119] More specifically, two questions are proposed; firstly, to what extent is an individual orientated toward maintaining their culture of origin, and secondly, to what extent do they seek participation (engagement and interaction) with the dominant culture.[120] Marc Bornstein cites these categories as the most widely accepted understanding of acculturation adaptation at the level of the individual,[121] although Berry also sees these strategies as extending to the nondominant group more generally as well.[122]

Firstly, *assimilation* is where the individual (or group) displays preference for the dominant culture at the expense of their cultural heritage. This is contrasted with *separation* where the individual or group is resistant to

---

115. Ward and Kus, "Back To and Beyond"; Ng et al., "Cross-Cultural Adaption"; Bornstein, "Specificity Principle"; Berry, "Living Successfully."

116. Berry, "Living Successfully," 695.

117. Berry, "Living Successfully," 697.

118. Berry, "Living Successfully," 704.

119. Berry, "Living Successfully," 704; Ng et al., "Cross-Cultural Adaption," 20; Ward and Kus, "Back To and Beyond," 472.

120. Berry, "Living Successfully," 704; Ng et al., "Cross-Cultural Adaption," 20.

121. Bornstein, "Specificity Principle," 5.

122. Berry, "Living Successfully."

engagement with the dominant culture and becomes more deeply embedded in their cultural heritage. Thirdly, *integration* is an adaptive strategy where the individual seeks the maintenance of their own culture in addition to desiring contact and participation with the dominant culture. Alternatively, *marginalization* is when an individual has lost connection with their cultural heritage but has also failed to connect and has even lost interest in connecting with the dominant culture, which Berry suggests can occur as a result of exclusion or discrimination.[123]

Although the perspective of the non-dominant ethnocultural group has been the topic of much discussion in acculturation, Berry argues that when used in its original anthropological sense it is understood as a reciprocal and mutual process. Hence, the four acculturation strategies of the non-dominant group are described by Berry as having parallel strategies related to the larger society. Subsequently, from the perspective of the dominant group *assimilation* becomes a *melting pot*. When *separation* is outwardly imposed by the dominant group it becomes *segregation* whereas *exclusion* is when the dominant group contributes to the conditions for *marginalization* of the group or individual. Finally, when the broader society accepts diversity and values the integration of non-dominant cultures, then *integration* becomes *multiculturalism*.[124]

Recognizing that acculturation occurs at the level of society and the individual, Bornstein distinguishes the changes which occur at each level. First, he identifies change at the societal level which "involves changes in social structures, service institutions, and cultural practice."[125] This relates to both Berry's theories and the phenomenon at the center of this study in a number of ways.

From the discussion in chapter 1, many have debated the form of multiculturalism developing in the Korean context with claims that the implemented policies and programs have emphasized the assimilation of female migrant spouses, in particular, into culturally expected roles rather than valuing their culture and potential contribution to Korean society outside of procreation and raising future citizens. This does not appear to fit with an understanding of multiculturalism where the diversity of ethnocultural groups is a widely accepted feature of the broader society. In contrast, Western countries, specifically Australia, Canada, the United Kingdom, and

123. Berry, "Living Successfully," 705.
124. Berry, "Living Successfully," 706.
125. Bornstein, "Specificity Principle," 4.

the United States, have longer "histories as immigrant-receiving societies which has led to similar national identities and conceptions of citizenship that are relatively open and flexible."[126] Due to their histories as receiving nations, these countries have a more developed discourse of multiculturalism which can be understood in the sense of Berry's use of the term.

According to Jatinder Mann in her discussion on multiculturalism in Australia and Canada, the multicultural policy which emerged in these countries "encouraged migrants to retain their cultures and saw this as a positive thing, as together with the Anglo-centric or Anglo-Celtic, a new national culture would emerge."[127] In the context of Canada, biculturalism and even bilingualism became an important feature of the multiculturalism which developed due to the influence of French Canadians.[128] It is important to consider however, that Mann reports the shift towards multiculturalism as occurring in the 1960s and 70s. This was a time in which she describes these countries as facing "a crisis of national meaning and a search for a new definition of national community."[129] As a result, multiculturalism has had a comparatively longer time to establish itself in Western societies who have been receiving countries for immigrants for longer periods of time. Even America where interracial marriage also has a complicated history, particularly between intermarriage between blacks and whites, saw increasing trends of international marriage from the 1970s compared to the development of the trend in Korea which, as discussed in chapter 1, has been traced more recently to the 1990s.[130] Of course this is not to say that perfect policies or a utopian form of multiculturalism has emerged in any of these cultures. The point is that they have a more developed and embedded discourse of negotiating multiculturalism than Korea, a society who has faced a more recent onslaught of immigration which has challenged deeply traditional family structures and practices as well as deeply embedded notions of homogeneity.

In addition to the ways in which acculturation involves change at the societal level, theories on change at the level of the individual have also been developed in various ways. Generally, Bornstein describes acculturation in the individual as involving "changes in a person's customs, habits,

126. Washbrook et al., "Development of Young Children," 1591–92.

127. Mann, "Multiculturalism," 484.

128. Mann, "Multiculturalism," 486.

129. Mann, "Multiculturalism," 497.

130. Zhang and Van Hook, "Marital Dissolution," 95.

activities, language and values."[131] Berry's theories on the impact of acculturation at the level of the individual are far more detailed. In addition to
the previously listed categories of acculturation strategies or approaches,
Berry lists two possible outcomes of acculturation for the individual which
are also related to the acculturation strategy that the individual is orientated towards.[132] Furthermore, adaptations or changes at the level of the
individual are seen as having cultural and psychological consequences.[133]

Firstly, Berry identifies cultural knowledge and subsequent *behavioral
shifts* as one possible outcome of acculturation.[134] This is generally viewed
as the less problematic changes which occur as the outcome of *cultural
shedding* and *cultural learning* where change primarily impacts the individual as they either intentionally or unintentionally alter some behaviors
to those which are perceived to be a "better fit" to the dominant culture.[135]
At times behavioral changes are motivated by cultural conflict at which
point an individual's behavior will change depending on the acculturation
strategy they draw upon.[136] For someone who is utilizing an assimilation
strategy, they will simply adopt the dominant norms, whereas someone
who is seeking separation will simply avoid conflict by withdrawing from
the dominant culture. In the case of integration, resolution of the conflict is
only possible once an outcome which is mutually satisfying for both parties
is found. Alternatively, from Berry's perspective, acculturation stress occurs when the individual is presented with cultural conflict which cannot
be readily resolved through adjustment or assimilation strategies.[137]

In the sense that prolonged exposure is thought to produce more problematic conflicts, acculturation stress is understood as occurring as a result
of continual interactions of diverse groups of individuals.[138] Even Augsburger claims that "mental illness rises as a consequence of rapid sociocultural change."[139] It has been argued that the focus on acculturation stress has
led to an association of immigrant mental health issues such as "anxiety,

131. Bornstein, "Specificity Principle," 4.

132. Berry, "Living Successfully," 207–8.

133. Berry, "Living Successfully," 704.

134. Berry (1992, 1997) cited in Berry, "Living Successfully," 707.

135. Berry, "Living Successfully," 707.

136. Berry, "Living Successfully," 707.

137. Berry, "Living Successfully," 708.

138. Im et al., "Acculturation Stress," 498.

139. Augsburger, *Pastoral Counseling,* 331.

depression, psychosomatic symptoms, identity confusion, and feelings of alienation."[140] Both outcomes, acculturation stress and behavioral shifts, are related to the four acculturation strategies, with assimilation orientated individuals demonstrating the most behavioral shifts and separation the least.[141] Furthermore, an integration orientated person who is supported by a multicultural orientated society is linked to lower levels of stress.[142]

In addition to understanding acculturation in terms of strategies and outcomes, adaptation can also be understood as occurring in the individual on two levels. "Psychological adaptation largely involves one's psychological and physical well-being, whereas social-cultural adaptation refers to relatively stable changes that take place over time."[143] More specifically psychological adaptation relates acculturation outcomes in terms of a "clear sense of personal and cultural identity, subjective well-being, and emotional satisfaction in a new cultural environment."[144] Sociocultural adaptation, on the other hand, is understood as reflective of daily functioning and social interactions.[145] A number of factors are seen as affecting sociocultural adaptation such as the extent of the diversity between dominant and heritage cultures, the length of engagement and interaction with the dominant culture and individuals within that culture, and cultural knowledge and competence.[146] Alternatively, psychological adaptation is described as being more influenced by "personality variables, life changing events, and social support factors."[147]

140. Berry, 1997; Berry et al., 1987; Ward et al., 1998; cited in Oh et al., "Asian Cultural Collectivism," 25.

141. Berry, "Living Successfully," 708.

142. Berry, "Living Successfully," 708.

143. Berry, "Living Successfully," 709.

144. Searle and Ward, 1990; Ward and Kennedy, 1994; cited in Ng et al., "Cross-Cultural Adaption," 20.

145. Searle and Ward, 1990; Ward and Kennedy, 1994; cited in Ng et al., "Cross-Cultural Adaption," 20.

146. Ward cited in Ng et al., "Cross-Cultural Adaption," 20.

147. Ward, 1996; Ward and Kennedy, 1994; Wilson et al., 2013; cited in Ng et al., "Cross-Cultural Adaption," 20.

2.3.1 The Specificity Principle of Acculturation and Anglophone Mothers

Recent developments in acculturation theory indicate that exploring the experiences of Western women as expatriate mothers in Korea will be a valuable contribution to the literature and the discussion on multiculturalism in Korea. Bornstein argues for a "specificity" principle at work in acculturation which recognizes details of context related to the individual such as *setting, person, time, process,* and *domain* as influencing variables of the acculturation experience.[148] In contrast to Berry's understanding of acculturation which assigns individuals to four categories of assimilation, integrated, separated, and marginalized, according to varying orientations towards maintaining and participating in the different cultures, Bornstein's theory takes into account the "many variations found among present-day migrants and their situations."[149]

Bornstein's theory is a tentative first step away from an established understanding of acculturation proposed by Berry. It "appeals to a moderator view that focuses on how key factors influence the size and direction of acculturation."[150] It has potential to complement Doehring's postmodern feminist approach to pastoral care which demands sensitivity to the context of the careseeker, but also in fostering an interpathic sensitivity to the personal narratives of the specific immigration experience of Anglophone marriage immigrant mothers.

The specificity principle of acculturation theory suggests the importance of individual and group differences to the immigration experience. Unfortunately, these factors have not always been taken into consideration when studying marriage immigrants in Korea. In relation to the government's treatment of marriage migrants, Hyun Mee Kim has gone so far as to argue that "Foreign women with diverse cultural backgrounds and desires are on the brink of being reduced to a homogenous social minority group."[151] Ironically she herself is talking only about the immigrant brides from within other parts of Asia. Coming to a similar conclusion, Keuntae Kim recognized diversity among marriage immigrants. Kim argues that "In short, the results from current analyses imply that married migrant women in Korea

148. Bornstein, "Specificity Principle," 6.
149. Bornstein, "Specificity Principle," 31.
150. Bornstein, "Specificity Principle," 5.
151. Kim, "State and Migrant Women," 101.

are not a homogeneous group. Rather, there exist substantial variations in terms of the socioeconomic conditions that the women and their family encounter every day, which is rooted in the intersection of multiple factors in the origin and destination country."[152] In other words, just as the specificity principle of acculturation would suggest, the experiences of marriage immigrant women in Korea are highly dependent on where they are from and their various social and economic backgrounds both in their families of origin and in their marital homes. Subsequently, contributing to the field by adding the experiences of Western women has clear benefits to the current dialogue of multiculturalism in Korean society.

In addition to considering the diversity among marriage immigrants, it is also important to consider how Korea as a country of destination influences the acculturation process. Again, this is reflective of the specificity principle of *setting* where a destination culture is understood to influence acculturation.[153] This is seen by returning to the studies comparing Korea with other Asian destination countries. Despite sharing some factors influencing the trend of "mail-order brides," Korea's context is unique in significant ways. In their research on the "mail-order bride" phenomenon, Junmo Kim, Seung-Bum Yang and Ador Revelar Torneo extend comparisons of "receiving" countries to other "tiger economies" in Asia such as Taiwan, Hong Kong, and Singapore.[154] In making comparisons among these receiving countries they fail to explore or even mention a significant difference between them. Taiwan, Hong Kong, and Singapore are all known for their strong historical connection to China, which although not absent, is very different in the Korean context and is evidenced in the language of these countries. They do however highlight Korea's resistance to immigration and their preference for homogamy and endogamy, or the preference for marrying within one's own culture and ethnicity.[155] Rather than being a minor difference, homogamy and endogamy are major factors which have influenced the particular narrative of multiculturalism which has emerged in the context of Korea. It will also potentially influence how marriage immigrants experience raising their children in Korean society.

For immigrant parents generally, there is a modification of parenting philosophies and practices which occurs as they are exposed to new

152. Kim, "Cross-Border Marriages," 86.
153. Bornstein, "Specificity Principle," 6.
154. Kim et al., "Marriage Immigration," 14.
155. Kim et al., "Marriage Immigration," 14.

approaches in the destination country.[156] A woman who is placed within the context of a family in that setting is arguably exposed to philosophies and practices at an even more intimate level than other sojourners. Furthermore, Bornstein argues that just as adaptation is influenced by exposure to the dominant culture, adaptation is also somewhat mediated through the immigrant's access to cultural enclaves which represent their culture of origin and the extent to which these communities are endorsed by the wider community.[157] Bornstein proposes consideration of these enclave communities as part of the wider specificity principle of *setting conditions*.[158] He demonstrated how access to these enclave communities factor into acculturation through providing the exchange of information and resources as well as a place to share and observe their ethnic festivities.[159] For the Anglophone mothers in Son's previously mentioned study, creating a family culture where children were introduced and exposed to traditions of both cultures was seen as an important priority which she articulated as "uncharted territory" for her participants.[160] She describes a phenomenon of "incomplete integration" where integration is seen as a process of adapting, exploring, learning, forgetting, and adapting over time.[161]

Other elements under Bornstein's category of *time* as they relate to enabling an immigrant to remain connected to their cultural heritage create an even more nuanced understanding of acculturation.[162] For example, Bornstein argues that an immigrant sojourning at a point of time when the development of technology facilitates communication with their culture of origin as well as making frequent temporary visits or long-term relocation to their country of origin faster and more affordable, also has implications for how the individual acculturates.[163] The frequency with which an immigrant is able to return home is related to class but also to living in a moment in history where frequent international travel is possible. Additionally, Bornstein recognizes that various communication technologies such as Skype are a reflection of the specificity principle of *time* given that we live

156. Bornstein, "Specificity Principle," 23.
157. Bornstein, "Specificity Principle," 8.
158. Bornstein, "Specificity Principle," 8.
159. Bornstein, "Specificity Principle," 8.
160. Son, *National Identity*, 648–49.
161. Son, citing Berry, *National Identity*, 652.
162. Bornstein, "Specificity Principle," 16–17.
163. Bornstein, "Specificity Principle," 16–17.

in a generation with greater access to other cultures.[164] Subsequently, he argues the need for acculturation science to further examine the relative implications of media and communication in the acculturation process.[165] He does however propose this challenge in the context of how media platforms facilitate acculturation prior to relocation, rather than in the context of remaining connected to enclave communities both in the host country as well as in their country of origin.

More specifically to the Korean context, as discussed in the previous chapters, although marriage immigrants are not the only form of immigration occurring in Korea at this moment of history, discourse is heavily invested in dialoguing about their integration.[166] As argued in the first chapter, the dominant discourse of homogeneity in the Korean narrative of multiculturalism would seek to categorize the immigrant mothers as assimilated or not in terms of how they are raising and acculturating their children, but the reality is more complex.

Given that Bornstein's specificity principle of acculturation is a new paradigm in acculturation theory, it has not yet been debated or developed extensively. It does however provide a useful framework from which to discuss Korea's current trend of international marriage that is impacting the discourse of multiculturalism emerging there. The contribution this theory makes to the current study is how it encourages and supports a highly contextualized understanding of acculturation, which not only complement's Doehring's postmodern feminist approach to pastoral care, but also Augsburger's description of an interpathic counselor. These theories are also implicated in the methodology and design of this qualitative study.

---

164. Bornstein, "Specificity Principle," 26.

165. Bornstein, "Specificity Principle," 26.

166. See Park et al., "Social Constructions"; Kim, "Global Migration"; Ahn, "Racial Project."

Chapter 3

METHODOLOGY AND DATA

In light of the absence of research specifically exploring the experiences of Anglophone women married to Korean men who are expatriate mothers residing in Korea, this study aims to contribute a phenomenological qualitative research approach to explore this phenomenon, asking the question "How do women from Western, Anglophone countries understand and experience raising a multiracial child in Korea?" This goal is consistent with John W. Creswell's stated purpose of a phenomenological study which is to "describe the common meaning for several individuals of their *lived experiences* of a concept or phenomenon."[1] Accordingly, the research consisted primarily of a series of semi-structured interviews which took place in March and April 2018 over a period of four weeks.

3.1 Research Design

This research follows a qualitative methodology as it is primarily outlined and described by John W. Creswell. More specifically, it predominantly applies a feminist research framework. According to Creswell, a feminist research approach often utilizes postmodern critiques which value the "importance of different discourses"[2] and social constructivism which seeks context specific understanding by relying heavily on participant's

---

1. Creswell, *Qualitative Inquiry*, 76. Italics added for emphasis.
2. Creswell, *Qualitative Inquiry*, 27.

perspectives.[3] Exploration of and understanding of the experiences of the women in this study were based on two primary assumptions which are consistent with recognized perspectives of this approach that view "gender as a basic organizing principle that shapes the conditions" of lived experiences.[4] Firstly, there was the assumption that the participant's status as a woman and mother in a society with structures of patriarchy and homogeneity firmly in place would influence their experience. In addition, this approach values women's agency and her ability to make choices.[5] Consequently, the second assumption which premises this study is that the individual participant's responses would be nuanced, valuable, and related to their context in addition to also having something valuable to contribute to the discourse of multiculturalism in Korea.

The specific qualitative methodology utilized in this study is phenomenological. The research follows Moustakas's transcendental or psychological phenomenology which prioritizes the "description of the experiences of participants" over "interpretations of the researcher" and utilizes strategies of reflexivity as one way of bracketing the researcher's experiences and positioning them in relation to the study.[6] This approach to phenomenological methodology also requires both textural and structural descriptions which refer to the "what" and the "how" of the participant's experience respectively.

The researcher was used as a key instrument due to matches both with the demographic of the participants and in having shared experiences of an intercultural marriage with a Korean man and raising a child interculturally in that setting. Creswell identifies the researcher as a key instrument in qualitative research due to their role in data collection including the interviewing stage, especially through the use of open-ended questions. On the basis of the previously mentioned shared experiences, the researcher had valuable access to this community but also additional responsibility for reflexivity and reduction. Reflexivity is the way the researcher seeks to situate themselves in various ways throughout the study by giving their background and experience and acknowledging the ways it has influenced their interpretation and understanding of the study. According to Amedeo Giorgi, reduction is "a necessary attitude for phenomenological analysis"

---

3. Creswell, *Qualitative Inquiry*, 24, 27.

4. Creswell, *Qualitative Inquiry*, 29.

5. Steward cited in Creswell, *Qualitative Inquiry*, 30.

6. Moustaka (1994) cited in Creswell, *Qualitative Inquiry*, 80.

and involves resisting prejudgment and assumptions of the essence of an experience.[7] As was outlined in the introduction, there was an intentional effort to achieve reflexivity which was evidenced by opening the findings of this research with a personal narrative. The following sections also describe the way that reduction was incorporated into the study, particularly in the data analysis stage.

Selection of an appropriate sample is also crucial to phenomenological methodology as "the participants need to be carefully chosen to be individuals who have all experienced the phenomenon in question,"[8] although this was notably less problematic to the current study than bracketing or reduction. The following section outlines how sample selection was executed and is followed by the demographic descriptions of the participants.

3.2 Participants and the Demographic Sample

The findings in this study are the result of a critical discourse analysis of ten interviews from a sample of women sourced from online social media groups. The participants were sought via posting on three major private Facebook groups for female spouses of Korean men, all of which the researcher was also a member. The members of the three groups variously self-identify as either Western, foreign or non-Korean spouses of Korean men, as reflected in the group names. At the time the request was posted the groups consisted of 981, 272 and 86 members respectively. There is however some overlap and movement of membership between the groups. Furthermore, as may be somewhat indicated by some of the group names, not all of the members are from countries where English is the national language. Aside from Europe, there are also some members from China or the Philippines given that selfidentification as Western and marriage to a Korean husband are the only criteria for membership. In addition, many of the members are living in their own countries with their spouses rather than in Korea, further making them an unfit match for the current study.

A post was placed in these groups in early March requesting participants who met a number of criteria. The post sought potential participants who would ideally be available for meetings in person around Seoul during a specific week in March, while offering assurance that it was possible to be somewhat flexible around that time even though that particular week was

7. Giorgi, "Phenomenological Psychology," 43.
8. Creswell, *Qualitative Inquiry*, 83.

preferred. It also made a request for women to meet three primary criteria. Firstly, they needed to be from "native English-speaking" countries. Secondly, they had to be raising children in Korea with their Korean spouse. Finally, they had to have no immediate plans to relocate back to their country of origin, although a vague plan or desire to return someday was considered acceptable. While recognizing that plans can and do change, the critical point was that they had to be planning to raise their child here for the foreseeable future. These criteria were set out in recognition of the influence that these variables could have on the acculturation process and experience as a whole as outlined in Bornstein's principle of specificity,[9] some of which warrant elaboration at this point.

Particularly, the final criterion is indicative of what Bornstein describes as the specificity principle of *setting condition*. According to Bornstein, "setting conditions of acculturation include reasons for migrating, place, experience, and status."[10] Although status and the culture of destination may remain constant with those of previous studies, the purpose of this study was to control for variables of culture of origin (to some extent), length of sojourn, as well as the experience of raising the child. According to Bornstein, all of these, excluding the latter, are factors which potentially influence the acculturation experience. In the context of this study, the knowledge that you would return to your country of origin in the near future can foreseeably have an impact on the overall experience if current circumstances were only considered as temporary. It can also potentially affect the level of engagement and investment with the host culture if the arrangement is considered to be more long term.

Within twenty-four hours of posting the requests, sixteen potential participants made contact. Of these participants, only one was not a member of the online groups. She had been notified about the study through a friend who was a member of the group and wished to participate. Without being more specific than the criteria previously described, the respondents were a somewhat racially homogeneous group with minimal diversity in terms of age, country of origin, and the number and ages of their children. Five of the participants withdrew from the study voluntarily before the interview for personal, scheduling or location reasons. Eleven interviews were successfully scheduled and completed although one was later withdrawn from the study, leaving a final data sample drawn from ten participants.

9. Bornstein, "Specificity Principle."
10. Bornstein, "Specificity Principle," 6.

After meeting and interviewing all of the participants, the decision was made to drop one of the women from the sample for demographic reasons. Aside from Bornstein's theory, according to Wodak and Meyer, various social demographic factors including race, ethnicity, and age are considered important variables in most critical discourse analysis approaches.[11] The initial request which was posted made no mention of ethnicity, requesting only that those interested came from Anglophone nations. This was with the expectation that some spontaneous diversity would emerge from the expressions of interest. Despite this, the sample of participants was surprisingly ethnically homogeneous. Of the eleven participants, ten were Caucasian while one was ethnically Asian and raised bilingual. One other participant did study in a French immersion school, however, this is also a different experience than being raised speaking a minority language in the home with minority parents. It was determined that the demographic differences with the previous participant were significant enough to affect the reliability of the sample, especially given the study's objectives to contribute the experience of immigrant spouses from non-Asian countries to existing literature.

3.2.1 Nationalities

The sample included women from the United States, Canada, and Australia. Of the ten participants being used in the study, five were from Canada, four were from the United States and one was from Australia (see table 2).

Although this is not representative of all Anglophone Western nations, it is somewhat consistent with the previously listed breakdown of marriage visa holders residing in Korea.[12] According to those statistics, the United States, Canada, the United Kingdom, and Australia represent the top four countries of citizenship of female spouses from Western nations residing in Korea.

3.2.2 Age

As well as representing a limited number of nationalities and ethnic backgrounds, the sample demonstrated a small range in terms of age. Despite

11. Wodak and Meyer, "Critical Discourse Analysis," 14.
12. See table 1 on page 12.

the age of women ranging from 26 to 40 years, only one participant fell into the 26 to 30 age bracket. Interestingly, of the five Canadian participants, four fell into the 36 to 40 age bracket. Similarly, all but one of the Americans fell into the 31 to 35 age bracket. The Australian participant was also aged between 31 and 35 years, making the Canadians in the study slightly older than the rest of the participants (see table 3).

The participant's self-selection in relation to this variable may simply be indicative of the fact that women of this age are most likely to be in this particular life stage of bearing and raising children. This becomes even more evident when looking more closely at the age of the participants and the number of children that they have.

3.2.3 Motherhood

The age and number of the participant's children is also relevant to their experience of motherhood in Korea. The sample displayed somewhat more diversity in terms of age and number of children than the age, nationality, and ethnicity of the mother. There was however still a relatively high level of consistency among the sample, especially as the age and number of children was not specified in the request for participants. The number of children ranged from one to three, although the majority of participants had two children. Of the ten participants only one had three children. Out of the three who had only one child, two were pregnant with their second at the time of the study (see table 4).

The children were all aged from infancy to elementary school age. In her study of twenty-five Anglophone women married to Koreans, Son noted that only sixteen women had become mothers and had children who were of elementary school age or younger.[13] She saw this as reflecting the relatively recent nature of the trend of international marriages in Korea.[14] The oldest child in the current study was nine years old with the youngest being seven weeks old (not including the two children in utero). Despite this age range, the majority of the children were of preschool age and attending either day care or kindergarten (see table 5).

Despite representing a range of ages of children, there were some similarities in the sample in terms of both the ages of the mothers and ages of the children. This was particularly true in the case of the participants'

13. Son, *National Identity*, 639, 642.
14. Son, *National Identity*, 639.

firstborn child. The experience of raising a firstborn through various milestones could be a variable in the overall experience of mothering in a host society.

All of the mothers except one had at least one child in Korean day care, kindergarten or elementary school. Two of the women were full-time stay-at-home mothers while another two were doing minimal freelance work once or twice a week. Another participant, although employed full-time, was coming to the end of the maternity leave offered by her employer at the time of the study. In other words, eight of the ten women were negotiating employment outside the home. Of those eight, six had some form of full-time employment. This indicates that the majority of the women were financially contributing to the household to some degree whilst raising their children. Furthermore, it also suggests that it is the accessibility of day care which makes it easier for the women to take employment opportunities. This is potentially important for two reasons.

Son found in her study that the Anglophone women's "relative economic empowerment" in conjunction with their "socially respected status as white, English-speaking foreigners, and their ability to live out their own culture to a certain extent" not only gave them a level of autonomy but also contributed to their overall satisfaction with their lives in Korea.[15]

3.2.4 Length of Marriage and Time in Korea

The length of time the participants had been married compared to their overall length of time in Korea is also a relevant demographic variable. Having lived in Korea prior to being married, giving birth, and raising children there, may not only influence their level of familiarity with Korean culture and society but potentially the way they process their motherhood experience. The length of marriages of the participants ranged from four to eleven years. The majority of the participants (70 percent) had been married for four to six years (see table 6).

In contrast to the general understanding from the current literature of the international marriage trend in Korea which assumes that the majority of women are migrating to Korea for the purpose of marriage, a large portion of the women in the sample had actually been residing in Korea for a notable amount of time prior to their marriage. Out of the ten participants, six had lived in Korea for a period of between four and six years before

15. Son, *National Identity*, 652.

marrying a Korean. One more participant had lived in Korea a period of one-and-a-half years before marrying; bringing the total of women who had lived in Korea prior to marriage up to seven (see table 7).

Even so, some of the participants do appear to have migrated to Korea as a result of marriage. Two of the participants had been in Korea an almost equal amount of time as they had been married, moving here to live with their spouse. Of all the participants there was only one who had lived in Korea for a significantly shorter time than they had been married. She had spent four and a half of their six-year marriage living in her country before relocating to Korea. Interestingly, this participant also cited the highest level of self-assessed Korean language proficiency of all the participants. Eight of the other participants all indicated their level of Korean to be "Intermediate" and the remaining mother cited her level as "Basic." Self-assessed proficiency seemed the most appropriate indicator of their Korean language ability, as it reflects the woman's experience and level of comfort and confidence in engaging in Korean society utilizing and communicating in the Korean language.

Table 2. Breakdown of Participants by Nationality

Nationality	Number of Participants	Percentage of Total Participants
United States	4	40
Canadian	5	50
Australian	1	10

Table 3. Age of the Participants by Country of Citizenship

	26–30 years	31–35 years	36–40 years
United States	1	3	-
Canada	-	1	4
Australia	-	1	-

Table 4. Number of Children by Age of Mother Participant
Note: An * indicates that the participant was pregnant at the time of the study.

	1	2	3
26–30 years	-	1	-
31–35 years	2*	3	-
36–40 years	1	2	1

Table 5. Age of Children by Birth Order
Note: The gap in age between row 2 and 3 is due to the fact that none of the mothers in the sample had a 6-year-old child.

	1st Born	2nd Born	3rd Born
7 weeks–16 months	-	5	-
20 weeks–5 years	7	1	1
7–9 years	3	1	-

Table 6. Length of Marriages

Number of Years Married	Number of Participants
4 years	2
5 years	2
6 years	3
8 years	1
11 years	2

Table 7. Time Living in Korea before Marriage

Years Living in Korea before Marriage	Number of Participants
Moved after Marriage	2
1.5 years	1
4 years	4
5 years	1
6 years	1

3.3 Data Collection

The data collection period lasted from early March to early April. After the initial expression of interest, contact, and interview scheduling, the participants were contacted again a week before their interview appointment. At this time, each participant was sent a copy of the participant consent form to review and a Google survey to complete before the interview. The Google survey requested basic demographic information such as nationality, age range, length of stay in Korea, length of marriage, number and age of children, and self-assessed fluency in Korean. The survey also sought confirmation that the participant had no short-term plans to leave Korea and asked if they were interested in being involved in further studies in the future.

The semi-structured interviews were all conducted in person. Each one took place in various coffee shops throughout the Seoul, Ilsan, and Suwan areas of Korea. The meetings lasted between one and a half to two hours with the actual interview lasting from forty-five minutes to one hour. Four out of the ten participants had their children with them for the interview with ages ranging from seven weeks to sixteen months.

After arriving at a coffee shop, drinks were ordered and paid for by the researcher as a gesture of gratitude for participating in the study. Whilst waiting for drinks, the participant consent form was discussed, and two copies were signed by both researcher and participant with each keeping one copy. The participant was reminded of their anticipated participation and rights to anonymity as well as their freedom to withdraw from the study at any time. The researcher then explained that there would be six general, open-ended questions which were designed with the purpose of generating consistent themes from the participants' responses, with minimal interference from the interviewer. At this point the researcher also explained to the participant that they were free to contact her at a later point if further examples came to mind and that they were also welcome to send other materials such as pictures, songs, or photographs if they felt like this would better illustrate or express their responses to the questions. Two of the participants later sent pictures and three sent messages with further responses to the questions. Finally, before starting the official interview, the participant was given the opportunity to ask any questions they may have had. To avoid interruption, the interview questions were not started until the drinks were received and both researcher and participant were ready. At that point recording began and the interviewer proceeded to ask the prepared open-ended questions.

The presence of the children had various effects on the interview. The younger children had less of an impact as they slept for the majority of the time. For the older two, and for one of the younger ones before he slept, the mothers were somewhat anxious about their baby's disruptions, but were easily reassured by the fact that the researcher was also a mother. They returned to comfortably responding to the questions amidst intermittent interruptions by their children after the reassurances. In one case, observing a mother interacting with her child actually led to a follow-up question about her use of language with her children which would not have been realized otherwise. She was the only participant to use Korean with her children almost exclusively.

The importance of reduction to the phenomenological methodology was taken into careful consideration even in the data collection stage of the research. This was particularly challenging as a Caucasian Australian married to a Korean man raising a three-and-a-half-year-old son in Korea while conducting these interviews. A conscious effort was exerted in order to allow this fact to contribute to developing rapport with the participant without allowing assumptions about similarities in experience to override objective judgment or disclosure on the part of both parties.

The researcher sought reduction at the data collection phase of the study in a number of ways. Firstly, it was achieved through beginning the interviews with an explanation of the rationale behind the broad and general nature of the questions which was to prompt responses. The researcher explained how the responses to these broad questions would be used to identify inherent themes with minimal interference from the researcher. Secondly, reduction was also achieved at the interview stage of the research through follow-up questions and sometimes by explicitly addressing moments when the participant brushed over parts of their description due to the assumption that the interviewer would have had a similar experience. This required continual self-awareness on the part of the researcher, and particular attention to moments when the experience of the respondent felt either overly familiar or significantly different. This was partly aided by the fact that 90 percent of the participants were North American rather than Australian like the researcher. Although all are Western countries, a conscious sensitivity to the possible cultural differences on the part of both the interviewer and the participant provided yet another avenue for reduction and distancing.

Finally, note-taking during the interview was another method used to achieve reduction. Throughout the interviews the researcher made notes of moments when the participant placed particular emphasis on an issue being discussed. As the interviews progressed, the researcher also made note of any spontaneous connections or parallels with responses from other interviews. This was a notable advantage of scheduling the interviews within a relatively close period of time as the interviews and initial first impressions were relatively fresh in the researcher's mind. These notes were elaborated on as necessary immediately following the interview either within one or two hours after completing the interview or on the evening of the day that the interview had been completed.

Each participant was asked a series of six questions with corresponding follow-up questions when deemed appropriate. The questions in order were:

1. Can you tell me about an experience you have had which defines or illustrates what it means for you to raise a multiracial child in Korea?

2. How do you think your ideas or expectations of being a mother have changed or adapted while raising a child here in Korea?

   • Can you give some specific examples?

3. What does the term "multicultural family" mean to you and your family?

4. What are some of the things that you consider to be advantages to raising your child here in Korea?

5. What are some of your frustrations or difficulties in raising your child here in Korea?

    • Do you have ways that you are actively trying to reconcile or counteract these challenges?

6. Is there anything else you would like to tell me about your journey and experience of becoming a mother in Korea?

The question regarding frustrations or difficulties was deliberately placed towards the end of the interview in the hope that by that stage the participant would feel enough rapport to be candid in their responses, which proved to be effective. Occasionally the order of questions was changed if the researcher felt that the content of the answer being discussed was beginning to naturally overlap into one of the other questions. However, for the most part, the question order followed a natural flow. For example, when discussing how their expectations or ideas of motherhood had changed, many of the women found themselves making comparisons between their country of origin and Korea, which lead easily to a discussion of advantages and disadvantages. Also, in following the natural flow of the interview, the researcher asked questions for follow-up or clarification based on the responses of the participants or observations of the researcher. One example of this was when the researcher observed the participant speaking with her child in Korean only. Inquiry lead to an insightful discussion of the decision-making process and rationale behind this language dynamic related to her intention for her child to be identified as a Korean citizen in the playground as well as her being able to teach her child to advocate for herself.

3.4 Data Analysis

The interviews were transcribed and cross-checked with the two devices used for recording. Once the interviews were transcribed, they were reviewed and listened to twice as a whole in order to gain an overall understanding of the content before coding began. Reading the transcripts "in their entirety several times . . . trying to get a sense of the interview as a whole before breaking it into parts," is a recommended first step to data analysis.[16] Amedeo Giorgi also outlines this as an important first step in data analysis. From this approach, the first two steps both involve reading the transcripts in their entirety; firstly, to grasp a sense of the transcript as a complete text, and secondly, to look for "meaning units" which reflect the psychological perspective and most clearly address the phenomenon at the center of the research.[17] After reading the transcripts for a third time in the process of identifying meaning units, the researcher also sought to summarize each transcript in the form of a short one or two sentence narrative theme. This was done as a provisional internal check to ensure that meaning units were consistent with the broad general tone of the participant's experience as presented in the data collection process.

Throughout the process of reviewing the transcripts, the researcher made notes of general impressions and experimented with mind maps containing the most overt connections between the participant's experiences and similarities in ongoing themes which initially caught the attention of the researcher. This was also later compared with the notes which were taken at the time of the interview in an attempt to keep track of how the themes were developing. Once the transcripts had been reviewed and meaning units identified, they were coded for major themes with particular attention being paid to similarities and parallels in meaning units which were raised in more than one interview. Attention was also paid to where the participant had used particularly emotive language.

From the data analysis three major, but highly integrated, themes were identified. These themes have been labelled *Functioning in Korean Society*, *Community*, and *Social and Cultural Identity*. The themes emerged through analysis of the interviews as a whole, rather than in relation to specific questions. The following section will describe these themes in detail using the responses of the participants.

16. Agar cited in Creswell, *Qualitative Inquiry*, 183.
17. Giorgi, "Sketch," 10.

Section 2

Results: The Experience of Anglophone Expatriate Mothers

Chapter 4

FUNCTIONING IN KOREAN SOCIETY:
Fluency, Wellbeing and Finances

THIS SECTION DESCRIBES IN detail the findings of the phenom-enological study outlined in the previous chapter. The three themes iden-tified from the responses of the participants are *Functioning in Korean Society, Community*, and *Social and Cultural Identity*. In the discussion of these themes each participant has been allocated a pseudonym to protect her anonymity.

The first theme emerging from the interviews with the participants covers a number of factors related to general *Daily Functioning in Korean Society* which includes the three closely integrated subthemes of *Wellbeing, Finances*, and *Korean Proficiency*. This theme articulated the various ways that the mothers understood and navigated the daily experience of mother-ing in Korea and highlights the various individual resources the women drew upon which are even more clearly elaborated and articulated in the other themes (see diagram 1).

**Daily Functioning
in Korean Society**

Wellbeing
- Sleep
(bedtimes/cosleeping)
- Air quality/environment
- Medical care for mother
(prenatal/postpartum)
- Food

**Korean
Proficiency**
- Communicating with
daycare/healthcare
professionals
- Sense of
independence/
being themselves
- Completing
daily tasks

Finances
-Government support
- Employment
(husband/own)
- Maternity leave
- Health care
(costs)

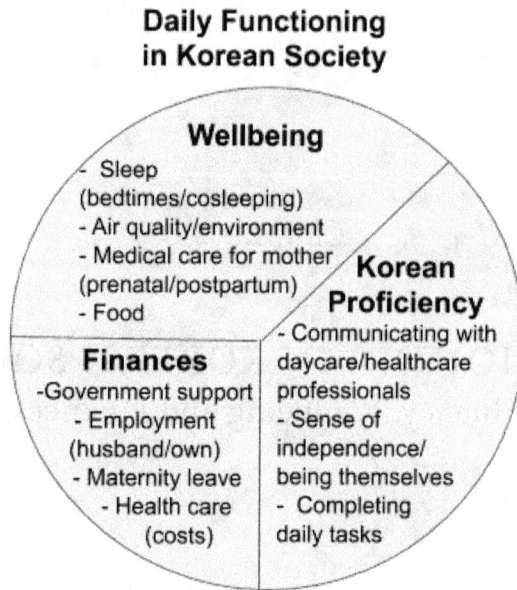

Diagram 1: Daily Functioning in Korean Society

4.1 Korean Proficiency (Fluency)

A recurring theme raised by all of the participants, which to some extent carried over to a number of other categories, was the issue of language proficiency of the mother. Again, more than any verifiable competency level, it was proficiency as it was experienced in day-to-day interactions that was primarily important to the study. For the women, their ability and confidence in communicating in Korean influenced many day-to-day interactions such as dealing with their children's schooling and receiving medical treatment for themselves and their children, as well as empowering them to be able to feel like they were functioning more as they would back in their country of origin.

Sue, who had the highest level of self-assessed proficiency of all the participants, saw a range of benefits gained through her ability to speak Korean. Some of these included reading Korean stories with her children, communicating with her daughter's kindergarten teachers, and helping to reduce the impact of her child being perceived as "foreign."

> I don't think I could overstate how substantially important it's
> been to my life to be able to speak Korean. (Sue)

In her experience of motherhood, this went beyond reading communication letters from the kindergarten and communicating with teachers. It also included her being able to understand what was being said to or about her child in the playground and being able to give her daughter examples of how to advocate for herself.

Whilst Sue recognized the impact of her Korean proficiency, others were also aware of the limitations to their proficiency and the benefits they would obtain if they were to improve. Visiting the doctor was one example described by the participants. Nicky claimed that in her communication with doctors the explanations of diagnoses were often oversimplified which left her feeling that her ability to be "as good of a mother" as she perhaps could be was more limited than if she were more fluent.

In addition to interactions with doctors, Jessica saw the limits to her Korean fluency affecting her day-to-day interactions in other ways. After detailing a shopping experience where she had felt embarrassed by a confrontation in a large store over the pricing and purchasing of a sale item, she recognized that the ability to understand more Korean would have helped in that situation. In this example her proficiency was secondary to her more significant feelings toward the incident and to how she had been treated as a foreigner. She had felt that her "foreignness" had drawn much unwanted attention to both the situation and to her. She described how the way she had been treated in the incident had been dismissed as a cultural difference, but she felt certain that a Korean would never have been treated in that way. Although describing these feelings was the primary purpose of raising the illustration, she recognized how her Korean proficiency also played a part in this incident.

Similar sentiments were expressed by Maggie who acknowledged that if she were to increase her Korean proficiency, she would then be a better advocate for herself and would be able to feel more in control in social settings.

> I could, you know, listen to a conversation and get all the nuances
> out of it but because I only sort of understand the conversation
> then I sort of wonder like, are they? Is my interpretation of what
> they're saying about me correct or am I missing something?
> (Maggie)

Justine saw her proficiency in Korean as impacting her ability to be as social as she would usually be back in Canada. Although recognizing her level was enough for her to get by in day-to-day interactions, a recent visit to Canada highlighted to her how much she had toned down a "deeply social" part of herself which reemerged with her ability to converse freely with everyone around her.

While recognizing and expressing a desire to be more fluent in Korean, many of the participants were also realistic about the practicalities that were involved in improving. They considered the current level of communication that they had attained to be acceptable while also recognizing the difficulties which could potentially emerge as their children continued to progress through the Korean education system. This was articulated particularly well by Charlotte for whom Korean language was less of a concern.

> I don't worry so much about language issues cause my kids kind of hold their own, and we, you know, we make, we muddle through with language stuff. My ability of speaking is good enough. (Charlotte)

However, Charlotte did share an incident where a day care teacher compared her Korean ability with another non-Korean mother from the Ukraine who spoke Korean fluently. The teacher directly asked her why her Korean ability wasn't as good as the Ukrainian mother. This had caused her to reflect on how difficult it was for her to improve her Korean proficiency while being a working mother. This sentiment was also shared by Justine.

> I would love to take language classes. I love studying but the time isn't there. (Justine)

Charlotte's children were the oldest in the study, having two already in the Korean elementary school system. Despite the fact that she felt that language was not much of an issue for her, a number of the mothers were conscious of the potential for language barriers to emerge as their children progressed through the Korean education system.

Although Charlotte did not feel too concerned about communication with her children's schools, Francis, the only other participant with a child in elementary school, did highlight the difficulties in keeping up with the large amounts of information being sent home from the school in Korean. With a self-assessed intermediate reading level, she admitted it was easy to miss details embedded in full pages of information. Not being completely aware of what was going on in her sons' schools was what came to mind for her as an illustration for the question of what it means to raise a multiracial child in Korea.

With her oldest child transitioning into kindergarten, Dianne recognized the potential challenges facing her Korean fluency as her child moved through to the higher levels of Korean education, of which she was already trying to manage by taking small proactive steps.

> I'm really nervous about being a, a mom of an elementary school student here and then a middle school student and then a high school student. But I kind of try to think like, just like day care's preparing her for kindergarten, day care's preparing me for kindergarten. (Dianne)

> I mean it's not the school system you're used to, it's in another language. So I think of this as my preparation as well. (Dianne)

For her this preparation meant looking over the notes written in her daughter's day care diary and reading it alongside a Korean book of short passages about parenting with her husband every night.

Jessica, choosing not to send her daughter to day care, had initially felt language barriers as her daughter entered kindergarten. She recognized the language barrier as being one of her biggest difficulties about living in Korea. She felt it limited her ability to communicate as freely as she would back in America, particularly when it came to issues concerning her children, such as schooling and doctors. She described how she wanted to cry when she first visited her daughter's kindergarten because she felt the head teacher had directed everything to her husband. Although he tried to translate as much as possible, it was his role as mediator which she had struggled with. For her this was strongly related to her independence and role as a mother. Being involved in her daughter's education by being able to understand and ask questions directly to the school was something she desired and expected of herself in her role as a mother.

To a lesser extent, Jamie was also concerned about her ability to communicate with her daughter's care providers. She acknowledged that improving her Korean language skills would enable her to get more than just simple or basic ideas from the day care about what was going on in her daughter's education. However, she also noted that it still hadn't concerned her enough for it to motivate her into making study more of a priority.

With her eldest son in kindergarten, Andrea also recognized the challenges in learning the Korean language which she was aware would become increasingly necessary to address as her children began to enter elementary school. Although she said she hadn't felt any "big barriers or difficulties," she expressed a desire and a need to be able to be fully immersed in studying Korean full time in order to improve her proficiency. Although she had utilized the home-based tutoring service available to marriage immigrants from the multicultural family center, and she had located classes to learn Korean for free, she still found it was difficult to improve because she wasn't using it enough due to English being the main language used at home.

> My husband and I are just in the, in the habit of speaking English at home that we just never use it [Korean]. (Andrea)

The choice of language used at home may also be a factor in the women's confidence and comfort in communicating in Korean. Along with Andrea, a number of participants, particularly Charlotte, Francis, and Justine, had made conscious decisions to make English the language at home due to the fact that their children were surrounded by Korean in their everyday life.

With a background in linguistics and having attended a French immersion school as a child, Justine had even discussed this with her husband due to her concerns of being the only English-speaking influence in her son's life. Like Charlotte and Francis, for them as a family, there was a recognition of the need for English to become a priority in the home because of their exposure to Korean all day in the community.

Interestingly Sue, who was the only participant who made a conscious decision to speak solely to her children in Korean, also had the highest self-reported Korean proficiency. However, the decision for Sue to speak to her children in Korean was also made in light of what was comfortable, familiar, and habitual, as with Andrea's decision. Sue moved to Korea from Australia when her daughter was around three and half years old after initially planning to live there long term. Having anticipated raising her child predominantly in Australia, she had begun speaking to her daughter in Korean when she was six months old in order for her daughter to have a grasp of the language. After relocating to Korea and discussing having her second child, she made the conscious decision to continue communicating with both in Korean.

> Because I already had sort of three years developed relationship with my daughter . . . I had to consider the fact that if I just switched suddenly to English, that's quite confronting to her . . .

and she's sort of at a stage of emotional development as well so it
didn't seem like a good idea to just switch into English. (Sue)

She also recognized the additional benefits this decision had in helping her to improve her Korean.

4.2 Wellbeing

The issue of health and wellness presented itself in various ways in the participant's responses, with Korea offering both advantages and disadvantages
to the participants' health and that of their children. It was also in these
day-to-day interactions where the women were most actively negotiating
and adapting in their experience of motherhood in Korea.

4.2.1 Air Quality and the Environment

Firstly, a number of participants expressed concern about the impact recent high levels of air pollution were having on their children. This was
especially highlighted in Charlotte's responses. She expressed how it was
becoming increasingly tiresome to have to constantly check the air quality
before going outside. She also expressed her concern and increased feelings
of guilt as she began noticing her children experiencing a greater number
of symptoms which she attributed to the higher pollution levels rather than
to viral or bacterial illnesses.

> Yes, we have access to pretty good health care and it's inexpensive,
> but I shouldn't have to keep going to the doctor for the same things
> because of air pollution. (Charlotte)

Similarly, Francis and her sons were already experiencing health difficulties related to the air quality which saw them regularly seeing specialists
every two months. She also lamented the way the air quality limited the
opportunities for her children to play outside which they would have if they
were living in Canada. Jessica and Jamie also expressed somewhat similar
sentiments.

Jessica described how the air quality hindered her from giving her
children the kind of childhood she wished to give them. This was illustrated
and emphasized by a recent conversation with her three-year-old daughter
who was anticipating the approach of summer and how they would be able
to spend longer hours playing outside. She described how in order to help

her daughter understand she had explained to her that they may not be able to spend as much time outside because the "air was sick."

Jamie's responses in relation to air quality also reflected how she saw it limiting her ability to give her daughter similar experiences to what she had growing up. At the time of the interviews she expressed how concerns over air quality were factoring into her plans to celebrate her daughter's upcoming birthday. She discussed how she was planning to hide eggs outside for her daughter and her friends to find as part of the activities as her daughter's birthday fell around the time of Easter. She described how this was something her parents had done for her when she was younger. However, she was aware that the plans could potentially be affected by air quality. She emphatically mentioned that the air quality worried her in a way which suggested that this issue had greater implications for her than the immediate outcome of the plans for the birthday party.

The women were very active in informing themselves about the state of the pollution with Charlotte illustrating her concerns with statistics from the World Health Organization on the amount of anticipated deaths in Korea which could be attributed to the air pollution by 2020. Similarly, Justine noted how the severity of the pollution was rising every year. Alongside the worsening air pollution, she also expressed a sense of concern as to whether or not it was irresponsible to keep her family there and expose them to the associated risks. She had also recently had a conversation with her husband saying how more than any other challenge or frustration related to living in Korea, air quality would be the only thing that would concern her enough to want to leave.

Charlotte also recognized that the severity of the air pollution was almost to a point where it was beginning to outweigh the many benefits she saw to living in Korea. Having a broad environmental perspective and consciousness which she had been fostering since high school, her concerns were not just limited to the air quality. When discussing air quality, she also talked about pollution more generally and expressed a desire for her children to be able to play in a clean environment.

The emphasis Charlotte placed on her children being able to grow up playing outside and engaging in nature, which was shared with other participants, also emerged as she discussed the benefits of living in the area where her family had purchased a residence in a villa. Although not stated directly, this implied a kind of childhood she remembers experiencing. She described at length how the location of their home afforded her family access to not only a large number of playgrounds, but a canal, which was surrounded by cycling paths and parklands where her family were able to see fish as well as dragonflies and birds. She also described how their villa was located near farmlands and was even close to a heron nesting reserve. Despite these opportunities, one of her major frustrations was that she felt dissatisfied with how the area was often polluted.

> I'm tired of the unclean environment . . . Going from an island on the Pacific Ocean with all the wood forests all around me and coming here, that's the hardest part of raising my kids. (Charlotte)

Air quality and pollution had also led to discussions of leaving Korea for Charlotte's family. Even so, simply leaving Korea with her husband and children was not a full solution for her given that many people she cared about would still be affected by it. For this reason, she was actively trying to educate and model both to her children and students in her workplace about taking care of the environment. She also expressed a hope that her children would be able to influence their peers in similar ways and that they would find acceptance as "good neighbors."

Dianne was making the effort to reconcile her concerns over the air quality in other ways. She expressed sadness over the quality of the air, especially since she saw the hot summers and cold winters as already limiting the amount of days which were ideal for being outside. However, she did not see that as being enough of a reason to move because she recognized that there were potential drawbacks to living in almost any place.

> I kind of think that if you just picked up and moved for that sort of reason where would you live? Because every place has its problems. (Dianne)

In conclusion, many of the participants were negotiating the quality of air in Korea, with some even expressing a sense of guilt over exposing their children to the potential risks as well as concerns over the ways they already recognized it was impacting their children's health. Furthermore, for some of the participants, frustrations over the ways the environment also limited the opportunities for their children to play outside also pointed to a deeper desire for them to be able to give their children a different kind of childhood or even the kind of childhood they remember experiencing themselves. Along with taking practical measures of purchasing masks and air purifiers, the women were deliberating how much the pollution affected their choice to stay in Korea long term and the quality of life they could offer their children. However, the women did recognize that living in Korea offered other health advantages.

4.2.2 Food

Although air quality was a health concern for many of the mothers, food was an area of culture which the women were actively negotiating with many of them, although not all, viewing it as a more positive element of their experience of motherhood in Korea. Many of the women recognized the health and financial benefits of incorporating Korean food into their family's diet.

Justine saw Korean food as being much healthier than the food she would be raising her children on in Canada. Aside from the benefits of it being healthy, she also saw Korean food as being cheaper and easier. As a result, she didn't see her family as blending the food aspect of culture so much as other areas of her experience. This was a sentiment reiterated by Charlotte who saw eating Korean food not only as part of her family's Korean identity but as a way of consciously "living off the economy" by eating Korean food which was in season. Her Korean nanny, who had become an adopted grandmother figure in her family, had taught her how to cook Korean food and side dishes. Francis, the only participant living with her mother-in-law long term, also ate predominately Korean food at home. She saw making the meals from scratch as one way she was adapting her motherhood to the context of Korea. Beyond the home, the Korean school system also played a part in the family's food choices as well.

The food offered to the children at day care affected the mothers in a number of ways. Jamie noted the quality of food her daughter was given at day care as a part of her satisfaction with the quality of care she received there. Similarly, as a working mother, Justine was thankful for healthy lunches being prepared for her son at school which she saw as easing some of her burden.

Dianne was actively learning from her daughter's day care of which feeding her daughter was one example. Dianne's daughter had started day care when she was seven months old and as a first-time mother, the day care had helped her in introducing her daughter to a greater variety of solid foods. Her day care had initially approached her asking if she wished for them to introduce her daughter to rice porridge. This led to her feeding her daughter more Korean food at home to a point where, for her, there was an obvious blending of culture in a way which wasn't necessarily as easy or possible in other areas of culture.

> The line started to blur between what was American and what was Korean because I've never been a mom in the States and I was learning how to be a mom here and I was learning a lot from her teacher. (Dianne)

Dianne's response highlights food as a point of adaptation and integration of cultures when raising children in Korea, particularly as it was mediated through the education system. Similarly, as part of her intentionality to create a multicultural environment in her home, Maggie sought to find a balance of different cuisines. For her, Canadian food itself is diverse and she is intentional in making sure that this is reflected in the food her son eats.

Food was one of the major things which came to mind for Andrea when responding to what it meant to be a multicultural family. She saw herself primarily adapting through food and had even started a Facebook group for other mothers cooking in Korea in order to share and exchange recipes. In the home, she integrated non-Korean food with Korean recipes which she learned from her mother-in-law and the internet. After the interview she recalled experiences of observing her husband adding the spicy Korean traditional side dish *kimchi*, made of fermented cabbage, to the table of pasta, garlic bread, and wine she had prepared. She also recalled herself making a shepherd's pie with *kimchi*, illustrating a very specific instance of combining a Korean food into a non-Korean dish. She saw her integration of Korean food very positively, as she felt her family were eating especially healthily in Korea. She had also had positive experiences of cultural exchange with food via introducing Korean dishes to her family of origin while she was visiting them.

For other mothers, the act of blending food had presented them with some challenges. For Nicky, this played out in two ways. Firstly, she recognized the difficulties she had in making choices about the food she was purchasing. She found herself limited in her ability to not only check the ingredients found in the food in order to assess whether it reflected her choices in what she wanted her child to consume but also her ethical concerns including how the food was produced.

Unlike some of the other participants, Nicky also didn't necessarily consider Korean food, particularly white rice, to be healthier. Subsequently, a second challenge for her was negotiating the emphasis that Korean society and her mother-in-law, in particular, placed on rice. She described one incident where she had argued with her mother-in-law who had been upset with her for feeding her son brown as opposed to white rice. Nicky had perceived the brown rice, which she felt she had prepared adequately, as a compromise by acknowledging the Korean dietary emphasis on rice while providing a healthier alternative to white rice. Alternatively, her mother-in-law had considered it unsuitable and difficult for her seventeen-month-old grandson to digest. This had led to the disagreements. Nicky did however note that this was perhaps just as reflective of a generational difference of parenting styles as it was a cultural difference.

Jamie mentioned the importance of food to the Korean culture and how important it was to what being a multicultural family meant to her and her family. She described how at the beginning of their marriage she had tried to prepare a lot of Korean food although the emphasis had shifted for her now particularly when considering what food her daughter consumed. This manifested as an active awareness of how much Korean versus Western food she had been feeding her daughter. She discussed how her husband would often request that she feed her daughter rice when he thought she had eaten too many "breads" that day. On the other hand, Jamie categorized breads, pastas, and rice together as carbohydrates and didn't feel the same necessity to feed her daughter rice as her husband expressed. At the same time, it was something she could easily compromise on.

> To him it's a staple and I'm not going to argue . . . As long as she's not having bread and rice in a meal then it's ok. (Jamie)

Rather than being a source of tension with her in-laws, Jamie recognized food as an avenue through which her parents-in-law tried to express their love and care for her and for her daughter. Firstly, she told how her mother-in-law would often bring over side dishes such as *kimchi,* which as mentioned previously, is another staple of the Korean diet, as well as other Korean main dishes. Her father-in-law also expressed his care in this way as he would often either call up and ask what her or her older daughter wanted to eat or would simply bring over a pizza because he knows it is a food she likes to eat.

Aside from food preparation for the family, there was also the aspect of food intake for the women postpartum. Admittedly this did not come up as much as could reasonably be expected given the Korean tradition of new mothers eating seaweed soup known as *miyeok guk* and rice every meal for three months after the birth of the child. This particular tradition was only mentioned by Francis and it was in a context of how her mother-in-law demonstrated care for her in a similar way to Jamie. Francis described how her mother-in-law had taken care of her for the traditional one hundred days after birth of which preparing and feeding her the *miyeok guk* was one aspect.

For Charlotte, giving birth in Korea positioned her between two cultures of which food taboos during breastfeeding was one illustration. When discussing how her expectations of being a mother had changed since giving birth in Korea, she explained how she hadn't even known that eating spicy food such as *kimchi* wasn't recommended while you are breastfeeding until she visited Canada with her first-born child. This all supported her more general point of how having children away from her country at a time when Facebook groups had not yet become as popular as they are now, meant she had a more relaxing parenting experience without any preconceived notions of the ways she was supposed to be doing things.

Subsequently, food was another aspect of wellbeing which the women described in their experiences of motherhood. It represented different things to different participants. Responses reflected perceptions of health, ease in preparation, and financial feasibility. In addition, it also became a form of communication or expression of care and, in one case, a source of conflict between the women and their in-laws.

4.2.3 Bedtimes and Sleeping Arrangements

Bedtimes and sleeping arrangements were another element of day-to-day life raised by the participants as a part of their motherhood experience in the context of Korea. Half of the participants discussed how they experimented with these aspects of mothering to differing degrees and reported differing levels of either positive or negative experiences with it. Many of their responses demonstrated an awareness of how variations of these practices were the expected norm in either Korea or their country of origin when discussing the arrangement they had eventually decided on for their family.

Francis and Charlotte had experiences which were similar in many respects. They both chose to cosleep and were still cosleeping with their youngest children at the time of the study. They also both chose to enforce bedtimes, although Charlotte had waited until her children were older in order to do so. Charlotte was aware that her decision to sleep with her children separately from her husband since the birth of her first child would be considered shocking to many Westerners. In addition, she saw it as more typical for Korean families due to the husband's long working hours. The long working hours were also the rationale for one of the compromises Francis had made in relation to bedtimes.

Although Francis had adapted to cosleeping she was more adamant in her decision to enforce bedtimes. Due to the children's protests, this was initially met with some resistance by both her husband and mother-in-law. Both had since expressed their gratitude after her sons had adjusted and come to accept the bedtime routine. Even in this decision there were still elements of compromise to Francis's experience. She had delayed bedtime to later than what she considered to be the norm in Canada in order to provide the opportunity for her husband to participate in some of the bedtime routine, allowing him to spend part of the day with his sons.

Interestingly, bedtimes and husband's late working hours were also mentioned indirectly as a part of Sue's responses but in the context of the first three years she spent raising her daughter in Australia. She explained that part of the reason she had chosen to start speaking to her daughter in Korean was because her child was already in bed by the time her husband was returning home from work. She realized that because of her husband's working hours it would be necessary for her to provide the majority of her daughter's exposure to the Korean language.

Just as Francis had been met with some resistance for her decision to enforce bedtimes (which she had done in conjunction with cosleeping), Dianne recognized her decision to sleep train, a combination of setting a child in their own bed, at a set time, also went against a Korean norm to cosleep.

> That's [sleep training] a little odd to my in-laws and Korean friends but . . . they mostly express jealousy that I have time after my kids are in bed although I know it's not what they would want for themselves cause they also, you know, have their reasons for cosleeping. (Dianne)

She also recognized this decision wasn't necessarily a choice to follow the American way either, noting that many of her American friends were not following this trend. Not unlike the gratitude Francis received, both Dianne and her husband had felt the benefits of sleep training. Although Dianne's husband had already been open to her approach to their children's sleep, he had become even more appreciative of it once the routine was settled and he was able to pursue other activities after their children were in bed.

Charlotte's decision to enforce a bedtime once her children were slightly older had hindered some of her efforts to befriend Koreans. When she would try to plan activities with Korean mothers and their children, she found that they would often want to meet after dinner and that the meeting would continue on until almost 9:00 or 10:00 p.m. This was a completely different approach to parenting, as Charlotte's children routinely begin bedtime between 7:30 and 8:00 p.m. while they can hear other children still playing outside in the nearby playgrounds.

In terms of cosleeping, Andrea and Nicky had opposite experiences. Due to the limitations of living in an apartment, Nicky had made the decision to cosleep with her son from birth. She found cosleeping to be a positive addition to her previous expectations of parenting in the way it had helped to facilitate a close relationship between her and her son. Alternatively, she did acknowledge her son depending on her to go to sleep as one drawback to the arrangement.

Like many of the others, Andrea had perceived that cosleeping was more typical in Korean families and was more familiar to her husband. As a result, she had trialed cosleeping with her first son but found it wasn't an effective choice for their family.

> That was kind of a different thing that I tried to maybe like, embrace and adapt to, but my first was the worst sleeper and cosleeping just wasn't that great. (Andrea)

Although to a lesser extent than other factors related to health and wellbeing such as food, bedtime and sleeping arrangements for their children were also areas where the women not only had an awareness of what were considered cultural norms both in their countries of origin and Korea, but were making highly personalized choices to suit their needs and the needs of their families.

4.2.4 Medical Care

Both prenatal and postpartum medical care of the mother was another element of the woman's experience of motherhood in Korea which emerged in various ways. Many of the participants mentioned the advantages of speed and cost effectiveness of the medical system in Korea but there were other aspects of medical care that contributed to their experience as well. Although when raising the issue of care for their children a number of the participants were primarily concerned with language barriers, communication, and comprehension of the medical needs of their child, a number of other issues related to health care such as choice emerged when discussing health care for themselves, particularly before and after giving birth.

In the discussion of their experiences of motherhood in Korea, both Dianne and Andrea expressed gratitude for the opportunity to stay in post-partum care hospitals in Korea known as the *Sanhu Joriwon* or *Joriwon*. A number of women in Korea choose to stay in these care centers for two to three weeks postpartum. Both Dianne and Andrea had stayed in a *Joriwon* after the birth of both of their children and had found it to be a very positive experience. Andrea saw it as advantageous to be able to rest and recover after delivery. Dianne believed that she benefited from her stay in the *Joriwon* by having an openness to the different infant care practices that she was exposed to which was part of her strategy for adapting to living in Korean society more generally.

For Jessica and Nicky, the benefits of medical care included having access to a large range of health-care providers. Jessica's access to choice for medical care providers meant she was able to find a hospital where she could not only communicate, but was given what she felt was appropriate attentive care. She described how she had moved hospitals during her pregnancy after one particular consultation with her doctor where the whole appointment had been directed to her husband in Korean even though she had been told prior to meeting the doctor that she would be able to communicate in English. More than a simple language barrier, Jessica lamented that she hadn't even been given the opportunity to ask questions as the doctor had simply told her husband to translate the content of the consultation after they left.

> When I was pregnant with Elsa[1] I was told that the doctor spoke English but I went in with my husband and it was all in Korean. Like, it was like I wasn't even there. (Jessica)

She was able to find a hospital where she felt more in control of the situation and eventually had both her children there.

> It was totally the opposite, whereas most places I was used to, like I'm just there but it's all for my husband versus like my husband

1. A pseudonym, not her daughter's real name.

was sitting there, like accompanying me, and they talked to me like I was the one in charge. (Jessica)

More recently, after the birth of her children, experimenting with health care was an important part of Jessica's independence. She described a more recent incident where she had visited a hospital with her husband but requested that he not go in to meet the doctor with her because she wanted to interact with the doctor without it being mediated through her husband in Korean. She had been very satisfied with the outcome. These seemed to be similar concerns that Jessica had in relation to her first experience in her child's kindergarten.

Considering that Nicky was pregnant with her second child at the time of the interview, it is understandable that she also appreciated the prenatal care she had access to in Korea. She recognized that were she to give birth in her small hometown in America, her choices would be limited to two hospitals. She explained how many of the expectant mothers in an online group that she was a part of who were giving birth in America were struggling to find a doctor they were comfortable with due to limited options. She contrasted this to her experience where she had continued to switch doctors up until she was twenty-six weeks pregnant when she found a doctor who could facilitate the natural birth she desired. Whereas Jessica desired to feel in control, Nicky's appreciation of the accessibility of health care represented choice.

I'm lucky that I'm in Seoul and I have all these opportunities. It's all about choice. I have all these choices. (Nicky)

Nicky also appreciated the affordability of giving birth in Korea. She noted that despite giving birth at one of the more expensive birthing clinics in Seoul, it was still far cheaper than giving birth in a hospital in America even if she were to have insurance. Jamie, having just given birth to her second child, also commented on the affordability of giving birth in Korea.

Jamie described how when she was pregnant with her first child, her husband, who was unaware of the cost of medical care in America, had suggested she return there to give birth. Recognizing that they wouldn't be able to afford the medical expense of delivering a child in America, she expressed her hope to have all their children in Korea before any plans to relocate there.

Out of the ten participants, two discussed their experience with postpartum depression (PPD). This refers to "depression with postpartum onset" as it is defined by the American Psychiatric Association. PPD is understood "as a depressive episode that occurs within four weeks of birth, but many researchers regard the postpartum period as lasting up to six months after delivery."[2] Various symptoms are recognized as indicating the onset of PPD including, "headaches, chest pain, heart palpitations, and panic attacks as well as fatigue, sadness, hopelessness, irritability, and loss of interest and pleasure in life."[3]

Justine experienced PPD for a period of almost a year and a half after the birth of her son where she felt a sense of loneliness and struggled with the loss of independence and her identity as a working mother. She did not seek out professional medical care but relied on online communities as well as using the internet to stay connected to her mother back in Canada. Although her parents were able to come and stay with her for four weeks after her son was born, she believed that the lack of a support system in Korea contributed to her PPD.

> I believe it was exasperated by being in Korea, where I didn't really
> have a support system. (Justine)

After the interview, the researcher contacted Justine again asking the reasons why she hadn't sought out professional help at that time. There were a number of factors which were related more to her personal disposition rather than living in Korea. The first of these was that she felt that what she was experiencing was a normal emotional response to motherhood which she needed to simply overcome. She also commented that she wasn't normally inclined to seek medical help for herself. Perhaps more specifically related to her Korean context, she noted that because of her short maternity leave, which was only three months, she didn't have the time to locate a suitable practitioner or have the time for treatment.

As a Christian, Justine regularly attends a church and at the time she had shared her experience of PPD with others in her congregation. She described how many women, both those who were mothers and those who were not, appreciated her honesty and candor.

> I always tell them, this is not everyone's experience but for me it's
> been, at that point I would say, unrewarding. (Justine)

2. Harvard Medical School Health, "Depression," 6.
3. Harvard Medical School Health, "Depression," 6.

Justine noted that the response from men was very different. One particular incident she had with her male pastor has important implications for pastoral care of an expatriate mother. Although her understanding of the stigma attached to being a mother prevented her from harboring bitterness towards her pastor, she described an incident where he had reacted negatively to her sharing her experience with another mother in the church.

> My pastor called me toxic for, for sharing my honest experience
> with another mother and he happened to overhear. (Justine)

Justine's experience of PPD not only highlights the need for sensitivity and care for new mothers who are parenting as expatriates but also the importance of their need for community which will be elaborated on in a later chapter. For her, online support, the developmentally natural growing independence of her son, and a parenting philosophy she came across which helped to reframe her interactions with her son were all pivotal in helping her overcome PPD.

Sue was the second participant to describe her experience with PPD after the birth of her first child. Sue had given birth to two children, her first in her country of origin and her second in Korea. Although she had PPD after giving birth to her first child while she was in Australia, her experience of receiving care does have implications for both care providers and the necessity of understanding the dynamics of acculturation. Whereas Justine was left wondering how her experience would have been different had she been in Canada at the time, Sue's experience demonstrates that cultural implications of motherhood in an international marriage are not necessarily limited to physical location as the specificity principle of acculturation would suggest. Unlike Justine, Sue did seek professional help for PPD after the birth of her first child but even so, found it very ineffective.

Sue felt that the care she received in Australia failed to grasp the multicultural aspect of her parenting. She found herself being given a number of suggestions which were difficult to implement in the context of her family with a husband who had a very traditional understanding of his role as a husband and provider. Specifically, she felt that they had overestimated the amount of support she could receive from her husband given the different understandings of mental health which exist in Australian and Korean societies.

> I don't think that in Korea there is as much of an acknowledge-
> ment of mental health issues . . . as there are in Australia, so the

amount of support that she would think that I could get from my husband is probably not reflective of how much he could actually understand what I was going through and, and be supportive of it. (Sue)

Sue felt that being recognized as different like she is in Korea alongside a general empathy toward the dynamics common to many Korean marriages could have been helpful, had she been in Korea. She attributed much of the lack of connection she felt to the advice and support she received from the counselors and social workers to a failure to recognize her context as being different and an assumption that her husband would necessarily assimilate completely to her needs and culture.

Whatever cultural sensitive, sensitivity training they may have or may not have, they cannot apply it to when they experience someone who is Australian by all senses but is in an intercultural marriage that, that it doesn't reflect their standard attitude of what marriage is. (Sue)

One example of this was when she was recommended to a mother's group at an early childhood center which consisted of all Caucasian mothers.

I'm also a white mum, but at the same time it also meant that none of them could understand the cultural things that I was experiencing in becoming a parent with a person from another culture. (Sue)

The overall context of her response implied that she felt she would have benefited from having access to a support group of Korean mothers. A number of factors such as *setting condition* and the *person* which Bornstein describes in his principle of specificity in acculturation[4] seem to be an important consideration in this illustration and demonstrate the importance of an awareness of these factors of acculturation experience when providing postpartum pastoral care for Anglophone women in marriages with Korean men regardless of their geographical location.

4. Bornstein, "Specificity Principle," 6–7, 13–15.

4.3 Finances

The participants raised a number of elements of their day-to-day functioning in Korean society which have been placed under the category of *Finances*. Many of the women saw financial advantages to living in Korea. Jamie, Charlotte, Nicky, Sue, and Dianne in particular all mentioned how much financial stability was afforded them while living in Korea due to the earning capacity for either/or both themselves and their husbands, the cost of living, affordable healthcare, and entertainment activities for the children, as well as government support. Dianne especially acknowledged how her financial resources had the potential to minimize daily frustrations and had contributed to her overall positive experience living in Korea.

> Money doesn't buy happiness but money can certainly help . . . I think creature comforts can help in a foreign environment (Dianne).

> If you have fewer daily frustrations it's easier to have a positive outlook. (Dianne)

More specifically, this section will explore the government support for childcare and experiences of employment for the participants and their husbands including maternity and paternity leave as these relate more closely to the themes raised in previous chapters, particularly in terms of Korea's concerns for low fertility and the influence of patriarchy in the culture.

4.3.1 Government Support

A number of the participants described how they had benefited from government initiatives for multicultural families in a number of ways. They demonstrated both an awareness and appreciation of these programs as well as selectivity and agency in determining which programs they utilized.

All of the participants appeared to be aware of the support that was provided by the government for day care, even those who were not utilizing it. Jamie even claimed that the government support for health care and day care was a large part of the reason she was content to remain in Korea for the time being.

Sue and Andrea also mentioned the access their families had to Korean language tutoring for themselves and their children. Charlotte had sought this support but hadn't been able to access it due to a policy which excluded spouses who had already been residing in Korea for an extended period of time. Francis, on the other hand, had been able to access one year of Korean classes through the multicultural family center. Once again, this demonstrates how a variety of factors specific to the circumstances of an individual can influence acculturation.

Sue, Nicky, and Jessica were actively choosing not to send their children to day care but utilizing many of the other services offered. Sue knew of the governmental provision for day care, however, she had instead chosen to keep her children at home until kindergarten and make use of an occasional day care service which could be accessed at a very cheap hourly rate. Upon request for further explanation as to why she didn't make use of the day care service, she responded that it wasn't necessarily particular to the Korean education system. Her decision was related to specific philosophies she had about the kinds of early childhood experiences she wanted to give her son. Keeping him at home was one way that she was able to provide and ensure that experience for him. She also recognized that financially it wouldn't be likely that her family could afford for her to stay at home with two children in Australia. Alongside being financially feasible, Sue also felt that having one stay-at-home parent was also more socially acceptable in Korea than it would be in Australia.

Nicky and Jessica were also aware of and navigating the limitations to government support within their families. Nicky had been searching for a day care which followed a particular early childhood educational philosophy she desired for her son. She had only succeeded to find a private English kindergarten but knew it would not be covered by the government allowance. Her husband had been against paying for day care and so she was still keeping her son at home. As with her prenatal care, having the choice to either receive a monthly stipend or send her child to day care was important to her.

Jessica represented an even more active awareness and negotiation of these policies. Having decided not to send her children to day care, Jessica had opted instead to receive payments from the government. She had recently returned to America with her children for an extended period and the government support had been a factor in determining the date she returned. She described how she had stayed as long as she could whilst adhering to the policy which claimed you are ineligible to receive the childcare payments if you reside outside of Korea for more than ninety days.

There were other day care provisions for multicultural families which the participants were also aware of which extended beyond finances. Jamie was able to develop her own business due to having her eldest daughter in the extended hours at day care which were offered to multicultural families regardless of the woman's employment status. Francis also described how being a part of a multicultural family also contributed to a point system used to allocate children positions on waiting lists in day cares and kindergartens. Andrea even commented that the accessibility to day care afforded by these policies, among other things, had even caused her and her husband to consider having a third baby.

> I think I wouldn't even consider that if I was back home because if I, if I had three kids at home that would be pretty tough. (Andrea)

Thus, these government initiatives to increase Korea's birth rate appear to be having at least some of the intended affect even on multicultural families consisting of an Anglophone mother.

Beyond day care, Charlotte described her interaction with government initiatives for multicultural families with elementary school aged children. Beyond language tutoring in Korean, which was available to the mothers, Charlotte had been exploring the possibility of having a *Damunhwa* or multicultural mentor for her two sons. While she was still waiting to see if one was necessary for her second son, she decided not to pursue the program for her eldest child after his teacher said it wasn't necessary. This decision was also based on her understanding that there were other multicultural families in her area who potentially needed these limited resources more than her own family.

Francis described a positive encounter where her and her family had been invited to an event for multicultural families through her son's school. She described how the Seoul Superintendent for Education had visited her son's school and given a speech in support of the children of these families, encouraging them not only to work hard but urging them to foster their difference. After the speech the families had painted a wall of the school together, taken pictures, and eaten lunch. This may perhaps be the kind of program mentioned in the introduction which is cited as being criticized by some for being empty governmental "displays."[5] Regardless, it was clear that Francis appreciated and saw a lot of value in her participation in the event.

---

5. H. Kim cited in Kim, "Daughters-in-Law of Korea?," 8.

4.3.2 Work Culture

In addition to the financial benefits afforded by governmental support, a number of women discussed employment expectations and culture to some degree as part of their experience of motherhood in Korea. Although Francis in particular had mentioned the late working hours of Korean men as a factor she negotiated in considering her children's bedtimes, the husband's employment had broader implications for many of the women.

Many of the women had a sense of the typical working conditions for many Korean men and evaluated how their husband's employment measured in comparison. For Jessica, her husband's working hours were tied to how her expectations of family life had changed by living in Korea. Although her husband made efforts to come home early, rather than the family evenings she had envisioned, he often spent the evenings working in the home office. In contrast, Dianne recognized the benefits associated with her husband's tenure position as a teacher which, among other things, had contributed to the general positivity of her experience.

> I do wanna acknowledge my privilege because I think I have a comfortable life here. And that has to do with my husband being a teacher with great hours, he has tenure. (Dianne)

Perhaps due to her pregnancy, Justine's discussion of employment extended beyond her husband's working hours to an awareness of the culture surrounding paternity leave. She knew that men were allowed three days of paternity leave at the birth of their child but recognized that stigma and fear of ostracization prevented many men from utilizing it. Her concerns, however, were not limited to paternity leave in a way which also reflects sentiments in Jessica's comments in particular.

> I wish Korean working hours and Korean workplaces were maybe, be more flexible in terms of, you know, allowing people work/life balance. (Justine)

For Justine and other women, this also extended to their own employment conditions.

Given that six out of the ten mothers were working full time in some capacity, employment conditions can be seen to contribute to their experience of mothering as expatriates. With a self-described identification as an "independent working woman" which had contributed to her experience of PPD, Justine also described in a number of ways how her employment had contributed to her overall experience of motherhood in Korea. Employed at a university, she was aware of the desirability of her position due to the low number of working hours, vacation time, and pay. She also recognized that she wouldn't be able to obtain a position like that in Canada at her level of education. As the main income earner for her family, this was a major factor in their decision to remain in Korea. However, this also presented her with challenges.

Alongside the benefits, there were challenges to Justine's employment experience. In addition to the shorter three-month maternity leave, mentioned by other participants as well, Justine also desired more job security than was provided by her employment contract which was renewed annually. Furthermore, she expressed stress over balancing life as a working mother and negotiating the division of domestic labor with her husband. Although there had been many discussions, they were continually reverting back to a dynamic which saw her in the role of "house manager."

> I feel like because we live in Korea and because of the very deeply entrenched gender roles here, it's like more, it's easier to just let that happen. (Justine)

Whereas Sue and Jessica were stay-at-home mothers and were not seeking to contest traditional divisions of labor, Justine's experience demonstrates that this was not the case for all of the women.

Dianne, also employed at a university, noted how her work environment had contributed to levels of anxiety in different ways. At the time of the interview Dianne was on maternity leave and so employment concerns did not immediately come to mind. After the interview, however, she did contact the researcher. Like Justine, she was aware that having obtained a position in a university, her working conditions were likely better than most, but she explained how a "heavy-handed" management style had contributed to her anxiety. The experiences of Justine and Dianne demonstrate the need to take into consideration the working conditions of expatriates mothering in Korea.

This chapter elaborated on the various aspects of functioning in Korean society which the participants of the study described as part of their daily motherhood experience. The next chapter describes the kinds of community the women in the study drew on.

Chapter 5

COMMUNITY:
Social Networks, Near and Far

ALL OF THE WOMEN in the study described the importance of relationships with both those in Korea and their country of origin to their mothering experience in Korea. For many, social media platforms were a crucial part of this with both Jamie and Justine spontaneously and independently describing Facebook as a "lifeline." Although the different forms of support networks the women had could be easily separated geographically, it is important to understand at first how the internet, and Facebook in particular, allowed the women to stay connected to both networks.

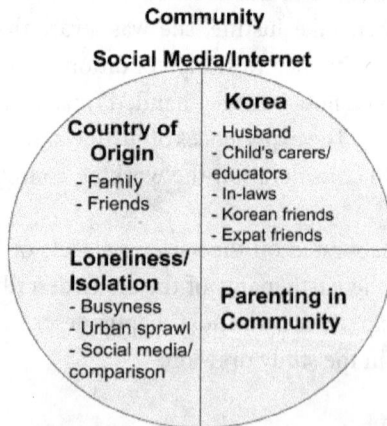

Community

Social Media/Internet

Korea
- Husband
- Child's carers/educators
- In-laws
- Korean friends
- Expat friends

Country of Origin
- Family
- Friends

Loneliness/Isolation
- Busyness
- Urban sprawl
- Social media/comparison

Parenting in Community

Diagram 2 : Community, Social Media/Internet

5.1 Social Media

Jamie's Facebook use was multifaceted in a way that her husband could not entirely understand.

> I wouldn't talk to my family and friends nearly as much if I didn't have Facebook. But he just doesn't get that. (Jamie)

She also described how social media is important not only in order to maintain contact with family and friends in America but as a platform through which she was able to become more deeply connected to community in Korea. As well as running her business on Facebook, she also sources information there, and valued the immediacy it offered not only in maintaining contact with her family and friends in America, but also for receiving encouragement and support when having a difficult day. Furthermore, as a Christian, she even recognized it as a platform for mobilizing prayer chains. She appeared comforted by the knowledge of the immediacy at which she could have a large network of people praying over her prayer requests.

Nicky also recognized the importance of Facebook in staying connected to her family while living far away, but also utilized it in other ways to develop her network in Korea. For her, the value of Facebook was in overcoming her more reserved personality to reach out and remain connected to a community in Korea. It was for this reason that she continued to use Facebook despite expressing a desire to quit it.

> I would love to quit Facebook, but I feel like at this point I need these groups in order to like, make new friends. (Nicky)

Joining online groups for women planning to give birth in Korea had not only provided her with a network of other mothers who had children around the same age as her son, but also provided a platform through which she was able to extend invitations to others which she normally wouldn't do given her more reserved personality.

> Because you can do anything behind a computer . . . You can have confidence and yeh, you don't care what people say. (Nicky)

Describing herself as a very social and outgoing person, Justine found a strong sense of belonging through the online Facebook community particularly via the group for women married to Korean men. As mentioned previously, online support groups of other expatriate women and mothers played an important part in how she navigated postpartum depression for a year and a half after her first son was born, especially as she did not seek out professional counseling. These groups were her primary coping mechanism to combat feelings of loneliness and loss of identity associated with PPD, seeing them as a way to connect with people.

Facebook groups also became a platform through which the women were able to meet and coordinate functions with other multicultural families and expatriates to honor holiday traditions which were important to them. Many of the women described their positive experiences participating in large annual holiday gatherings with other expatriate families to celebrate Easter and Halloween which were planned primarily through Facebook. As the interviews were scheduled around the time of Easter, many of the participants had plans to participate in one of the Easter egg hunts which were planned around Seoul with their children. For Andrea it was important that her sons partake in these kinds of traditions, but she recognized it was challenging to find ways to do this when they weren't being practiced more broadly in the community. This was one of the reasons she enjoyed participating in these events. Francis also recognized the importance of community to celebrating these cultural aspects of Easter as well as Halloween.

Charlotte played a key role in coordinating one of the Halloween events which is attended by approximately fifty or more families annually.

> We trick or treat in the park and we set up mats and bring candy
> and I do some songs and chant and we decorate. (Charlotte)

After the interview, Maggie sent a series of pictures which she felt illustrated her experience of raising her son in Korea. One of these pictures depicted her son and his friend dressed in a costume participating in one of these Halloween events. Andrea not only enjoyed watching her sons get excited for Halloween through attending events but utilized children's cartoons such as Paw Patrol to reinforce and bring context to the experience for her children.

> I feel like it's awesome that he was able to experience the Hallow-
> een because now when he watches it, he can relate his experience
> to what he's watching and he can understand it. (Andrea)

It was the aspect of recreating the feelings of anticipation and excitement surrounding the holidays which were a part of her childhood memories that was significant for Andrea. These events were an avenue where she could accomplish this. This demonstrates the importance of these large events to these women but also how they were utilizing them to share and teach their children their cultural traditions.

The women in the study also utilized the Facebook groups to assist them in celebrating the holidays from their culture in more intimate gatherings. Justine had even posted an open invitation in one of the Facebook groups to invite people to celebrate Christmas at her home. She noted how the online connections she had made had become friends in real life through various events or scheduled meet-ups. Francis also celebrated Christmas with multicultural families she had met online where they gathered in a home, shared a meal, cake, and the children exchanged gifts.

Similarly, Dianne had formulated a circle of friends of other multicultural families with a Western mother through the Facebook group with whom she had created new holiday traditions. For the past three years they had celebrated "ThanksgivaChristmas" in between the American Thanksgiving and Christmas where they shared a potluck meal together. Formulating these new holiday traditions rather than trying to replicate her own childhood experiences was an intentional decision Dianne had made. She recognized that trying to replicate all of her traditions would only lead to disappointment for her due to the amount of effort creating those American traditions required of the whole family.

> I don't try to burden myself to make American holidays feel like they would feel in America because I think it takes a whole family to do that. (Dianne)

> I think it's just setting yourself up for misery and discontent to even try you know? (Dianne)

This was very different to Andrea's emphasis on recreating the feeling of the holidays.

Maggie's experience demonstrates another way that the women were utilizing the internet to not only stay connected to community but also to honor their holiday traditions. Another one of the pictures she sent showed her son opening an Advent calendar window in front of a computer. Her mother could be seen on the screen watching via video chat as her grandson participated in this Christmas tradition which they celebrate in Canada. It was a way she could be involved in and connected to her grandson's enjoyment of the tradition which she had facilitated by sending the Advent calendar from Canada.

Andrea utilized the Facebook groups to celebrate holidays in other ways besides keeping up with the holiday celebrations. She searched these groups to locate the items she needed for the celebrations which weren't readily available in Korea. With Easter approaching, she found information online about where she could order the plastic Easter eggs, which are often used in Easter egg hunts in America but not commonly sold in stores in Korea.

As well as providing a platform through which these women could find support and celebrate their traditions, the online community also became a channel through which they could find a form of empowerment and regain a sense of their former self. This was also related to the holiday celebrations. For example, Justine felt that the big Halloween and Easter holiday events, which were organized by those in the expatriate community using the groups, also provided an outlet for her social personality. This was important particularly as she felt this was sometimes hindered due to living in Korea. Using these celebrations as a social outlet for her outgoing personality was just as important to her as the aspect of observing the traditions.

> I feel like when I, I commit to it, and when I'm preparing for it, it's for my son you know? And I do a lot of preparation, but once I get there and, you know, I see people and I start talking to people, then it's like . . . I don't really worry too much about like the actual egg hunt or the actual costumes . . . I very quickly kind of revert into my old, you know, social self. (Justine)

Furthermore, Justine also found the groups had become a channel for her to help others which she also described as another innate part of her personality that she felt was hindered by the language barrier while living in Korea. Helping people as a way of developing a sense of community was another aspect which was facilitated through the Facebook groups described by Jamie. She shared how she had seen women in Korea escape abusive situations using these Facebook groups. By responding to a post on one of these groups from someone requesting potting soil she had come into contact with another foreigner in her area.

> You know, I never in a million years would have met them or gotten them to take some potting soil from me had it not been for a random social media platform. (Jamie)

Although the language barrier sometimes hindered her daily life in Korea, Jessica found a sense of empowerment through the Facebook groups as well. For her this was a way to regain a sense of her independence. She used Facebook groups to source information for everything from craft supplies, sales on grocery items, different festivals and events, to doctors and dentists for her children and herself. Sourcing this information from the online community had empowered her to become more independent and less reliant on her husband.

> I'm seeing it all on different Facebook groups so that's really helped 'cause it makes me feel like I'm more knowledgeable about what's going on here. (Jessica)

A couple of times throughout the interview, she mentioned how her husband often jokingly commented on how she "was more in the know" about some aspects of life in Korea which she attributed to the information she had obtained through these groups. Because Jessica had relocated to Korea after marriage, finding this "web" of people she could draw on for recommendations as well as information had made a huge difference to her current experience compared to when she had first arrived in Korea.

Francis and Jamie had very different experiences in combining the different information they found on the Facebook groups with their husband's support. As mentioned previously, Jamie's husband disliked her dependence on social media and often didn't trust the information she sourced there. In contrast, like Jessica, Francis's husband was more supportive. She would often ask him to search for more information online in Korean after she had heard about some benefits such as the day care admission point system.

In their discussion on how they utilized Facebook, many of these women demonstrated sensitivity to the risks associated with the platform. Both Nicky and Justine expressed a desire to disconnect from Facebook due to the negativity they saw there but recognized that they were unlikely to disconnect in reality. Nicky cited the negativity and debates posted by her American contacts over current issues in the United States, such as the Trump administration and gun control, as a major reason she desired to quit social media. For Justine and others their observations were more related to the expatriate community in Korea.

Justine believed there were benefits to the negativity seen in the Facebook groups. Although she personally tried to limit herself from sharing too many of her own negative experiences, she did have moments when she had benefited from doing so.

> There have been a couple of times when I have. When I've really been kind of beyond and I've just felt like it's just been such a wonderful release and the women are so supportive. (Justine)

Aside from being a personal outlet, she also found encouragement from knowing that she wasn't alone in experiencing difficult times when she did read some more negative posts.

Dianne and Andrea however were highly selective in their interactions with social media. Facebook was a platform which could be either really positive or really negative according to Dianne. Recognizing her sensitivity to certain information, she saw her selectivity as an important way to maintain a sense of positivity and control over her mind while living in Korea. She was aware that her experience and life in Korea appeared more positive than many others whose experiences she read about in the Facebook groups. She had also begun to realize the influence that some of these negative experiences had started to have on her.

> I would let one person's experience carry more weight than it should you know? (Dianne)

After reading these posts she would start to question her happiness as well as begin to generalize about the negative behavior of Korean men as a group. She reached a point, however, where she realized that there was perhaps a negative bias towards the stories shared on Facebook and that she should become more selective in what she read.

> I think when I realized who writes on Facebook? Do happy people update everyone with the happiest events of their lives on Facebook? Yeh kind of . . . but also do like the saddest people who are isolated and don't have many friends go to Facebook to vent and hear from other people? You know? I mean, maybe the well-adjusted people with the positive stories, maybe they're just not gonna be found on Facebook because they have no need for Facebook in that way. (Dianne)

Andrea also was selective in how she used the Facebook groups in order to avoid the negativity. As mentioned previously, she had created a group where she could exchange recipes for children with other mothers. Rather than following the discussion threads on Facebook, she usually limited her interactions with the various groups she was a part of to when she was searching for items or in order to request information.

> I actually don't follow them because a lot of the times I find that if I read what everyone else is talking about it can be a lot of drama. (Andrea)

Similar to Dianne, she would stop following and reading discussions in a group when she felt the content was becoming too negative or there was a large amount of complaining. Even so, she saw the drama she observed as more reflective of the whole Facebook platform in general, rather than being specific to the geographical location or expatriate experience of the members.

> But I think every group can be like that, whether it's where you are. It's just how Facebook can be sometimes. (Andrea)

On the other hand, Charlotte saw the "drama" associated with the online community not only spill over into real-life interactions but saw it as being exasperated by the expatriate experience.

5.2 Maintaining Friendships Near and Far

Charlotte had seen the online drama many of the women described extend over from the online community into real-life relationships to some extent. Although she viewed Facebook as a platform which allowed women to form strong and lasting friendships, she also saw it work the opposite way. She described how often the intense need for connection sometimes brought together some mothers who perhaps wouldn't have been friends if they were in their country of origin due to different parenting philosophies. After initially intense connections based on mutual status as foreigners married to Koreans with children, she would see these same friendships dissolve after the friends realized that they had very little else in common. This became further complicated due to the small size of the expatriate community.

> It's a small community so you still have to maintain contact so it can be awkward and still isolating. (Charlotte)

Dianne's responses in particular demonstrate the necessity these women saw in being selective about their online community. Recognizing the challenges that distance created to relationships, Dianne was intentional about the relationships she invested in. She purposefully worked at building on relationships with friends who lived in her area and those in particular who had a more long-term plan to stay in Korea. Connecting with other expatriates and Koreans in her area was an important way for her to feel a part of a community and to avoid the extra energy required to maintain friendships with those who lived further away.

> I don't think it's good to meet people and then just keep meeting up with every expat you've met and kind of spreading yourself too thin and traveling really far to meet them. I mean I think it's great when you find people you have a real connection with in your city. (Dianne)

Dianne's approach to friendship was part of an overall strategy and philosophy she had toward living as an expatriate. She was purposeful about "celebrating where you are" rather than longing to be somewhere else. This extended beyond friendships, to how she celebrated holidays, and even to how she decorated her home. It was the decision she had made with her husband to settle in Korea that had made these things easier and contributed to the overall satisfaction she had experienced living there.

5.3 Loneliness

Many of the women described feelings of isolation and loneliness as part of their experience of mothering as an expatriate, which was expressed in various ways by many of the participants. As a social person, Justine even described loneliness as her greatest fear.

Although Francis's children were older now, she described how it was easy to feel lonely, particularly as a first-time mother in Korea. With her children progressing through the Korean education system and now developing their own interests, she felt less of a need for the expatriate community. However, she did note that this was also due to the busyness of her schedule as a working mother and the fact that a number of her friends had moved away. She remembered how important the expatriate community was particularly as a first-time mother. Aside from the support needed when facing the many questions and concerns which naturally arise when you first have a child, she felt mothers also needed community in order to socialize their children. For this reason, she felt it was necessary for expatriate mothers to support each other through mother's groups and meet-ups particularly early in their motherhood. She also noted how the feelings of loneliness could be particularly difficult for those who resided outside of Seoul which made it difficult for them to meet up with an expatriate community. The experience of others, however, demonstrates that living in Seoul itself was not necessarily enough.

For Charlotte and many others, the busyness of being a working mother in conjunction with the urban sprawl of Seoul made maintaining relationships difficult. She described how this had also impacted her daughter, who had lost connection with one of her earliest best friends due to the difficulties in scheduling time for them to meet. It was through this illustration that one motivation behind a dominant narrative of Charlotte's interview emerged. Charlotte talked often throughout her interview about her goal of raising "good Koreans." She used the story of how her daughter had lost the connection with her friend's daughter, to explain why she focuses so much on raising her children with a strong grounding in Korean culture.

> That's the other reason I try to raise them Korean, so that they can have more Korean friends . . . and play in our neighborhood and know their neighbors. Um, it's easier for them to have local friends even if I don't. My children still have somebody they can connect with. (Charlotte)

Charlotte's experience demonstrates a concern that the mothers had with building a sense of community for their children as well as the importance many of the women placed on the development and acceptance of their children's Korean identity which will be elaborated on in a later chapter.

For some of the women, feelings of loneliness were attributed to longing for more of a connection with their friends back in their country of origin, particularly around the timing of significant events. Having a more reserved personality, Nicky described missing her friends back home. Recently she had experienced feelings of sadness as she wasn't able to celebrate her pregnancy and the birth of her second child as she would in America by having a baby shower with her friends. Christmas was also particularly difficult for her. This was more for the social aspect of the celebrations as she appreciated being away from the materialism of the holiday which she saw in many of the American Christmas traditions. Some of her closer friends she had made in Korea had either moved further away or were busy, which made it difficult when special occasions arose. As a result, she had tried to introduce some Christmas festivities to her husband's friends and this had been well received.

Just as Facebook had been used to create a sense of community, it had also in some ways contributed to Charlotte's feelings of loneliness and isolation. Her feelings of isolation extended to when she would observe a friendship history unfold between people back in Canada. In a jokingly wistful way, she described observing friends in Canada not only maintain their friendships together, but the transfer of those strong relationships into close friendships between their children and even their husbands. However, Justine's experience of visiting friends back home suggests that this idealization of the connections they observed on Facebook may not necessarily be the reality.

Justine had recently returned to Canada after feeling burned out by her life in Korea. During that time, she had been enjoying a gathering with a group of close friends and had expressed to them her desire to live closer so that they could meet up more frequently. They had all responded how this gathering was not a regular occurrence due to the fact that the majority of them also have families and there are difficulties in scheduling time to meet up. Nicky also described a memorable gathering with a group of three of her closest friends who had all flown in from different parts of America to spend the weekend together at the beach when she had visited the previous year. These experiences demonstrate that despite an idealization of being close to friends in their country of origin, the reality was that due to the distance, extra effort to connect was made when they were able to visit. This was a way that the women were able to reconcile the distance from their friends. Many of the women also recognized this reality while being away from their family of origin as well.

5.4 Family

While Facebook and the internet allowed the women to stay connected to their families and friends in their countries of origin, many of them expressed a desire to be closer to their families for the additional support. They expressed various ways in which they reconciled this desire.

Dianne, like others such as Justine, expressed a desire to be closer to her family to be able to draw on them for additional support. She envisioned being more comfortable asking for support such as babysitting or benefiting from the ability to be able to simply go to her family home to relax and have a meal when she felt overly tired. She reconciled this desire by acknowledging the fact that even if she were to return to America with her family, there would be no guarantee that employment opportunities for her and her husband would allow her to live close by. Her second rationale for accepting the distance with her family was her ability to return home somewhat frequently, a factor reflected in the responses of other participants as well.

Whereas Maggie, Justine, and Francis expressed their frequent visits home as an opportunity to ground or reemerge themselves and their children in their culture, Andrea and Dianne saw their visits as affording them quality time with their families both for themselves and their child in a way which balanced out the rest of the year when they were separated. Although she wasn't able to enjoy the day-to-day encounters and comforts afforded by living close to her parents, Dianne appreciated being able to spend vacation time with her family which she felt eventually added up to more time given they were together for almost the entirety of her visit.

Andrea was realistic about the individualistic nature of her family and how that dynamic would work if they were to live in Canada. She reasoned that moving to Canada would not necessarily equal more time for herself, her children, and her family. She felt that she was afforded more family support from her in-laws due to living in Korea. Given that her brother and his family weren't living in the same state as their mother, the two months she returned home afforded her and her children more time with her mother than her brother's family received. She observed that the relationship her mother had with her grandchildren, including the ones living in Canada, wasn't as involved to the same extent as the relationship she saw between her children and her in-laws. As a result, Andrea described her relationship with her in-laws very positively. This relationship and the support Andrea received from her parents-in-law in raising her children was one of the advantages she saw to raising her children in Korea. The close relationship between her sons and their Korean grandparents is one of the reasons she loves living in Korea.

Although it was not asked directly in the interview questions, some of the women referenced their relationship with their mother-in-law as it had impacted their experience of parenting in Korea. Many of the women's responses suggested an awareness of the stereotypes of the tense relationships between mother-in-law and daughter-in-law in Korean culture. Whereas Nicky mentioned tensions with her parents-in-law related to differences in parenting philosophies particularly surrounding food, many of the other participants described their interactions with their mother-in-laws differently. Contrary to the stereotypical tensions, they either expressed gratitude for their support like Andrea, or commented on how they had assumed their mother-in-laws would be more involved.

Francis was the only participant in the study who lived with her mother-in-law as part of a permanent arrangement. While she told how there had been challenges and disagreements mostly after the birth of her children, she also described deep gratitude and mutual love and care. As mentioned previously, part of this conflict had been surrounding the issue of bedtimes. At the time of this disagreement, Francis had asserted authority in her role as mother, in order to convince her husband and mother-in-law.

Francis also described the benefits of living with her mother-in-law. She had seen and appreciated how the relationship between her children and their aging, widowed grandmother had fostered their empathy and compassion, but also how her mother-in-law had supported her through her motherhood journey. In a similar way to Dianne, Francis saw the importance of learning from Korean culture. In addition, when her sons were younger, Francis had experienced a period of severe anxiety while studying for her master's degree. This episode of anxiety had at the time left her unable to leave the house. She had been able to overcome that season with the support of her mother-in-law who had taken care of picking up and dropping off her son to day care.

For Francis, a sense of responsibility to her mother-in-law was one of the major factors preventing her from relocating back to Canada. Francis desired to move her family back to Canada particularly due to the increasingly poor air quality; however, the decision to move was complicated by a sense of responsibility for her mother-in-law. Francis's mother-in-law had said she did not wish to move to Canada if Francis were to relocate with her husband and children. Given that Francis's husband was her widowed mother-in-law's only child, this would leave her alone in Korea. It is both concern and care alongside feelings of guilt due to how much her mother-in-law had given to her family which keeps her from moving. She expressed her understanding of her feelings of guilt in a way which was somewhat cultural.

> But it's like that Korean mother thing you know? When she gives too much and then you feel guilty your whole life. It's like you have to give it back, I think. All Koreans feel that. Don't they? (Francis)

Although the relationship Francis described with her mother-in-law was emotive, it was feelings of mutual care and concern, and conflicting needs which were the source of the tension.

Whereas Andrea and Francis, in particular, expressed how their experiences of motherhood had been positively influenced by the support offered by their in-laws, others expressed an expectation that their mothers-in-law in particular would be more involved with their children. Sue had initially expected support from her mother-in-law to be one of the benefits of relocating to Korea with her daughter. After she had moved, however, she had found it disappointing that despite living so close, her mother-in-law was not willing to help more with her children. This was despite the fact that she lived five minutes away from her mother-in-law at the time of the interview. Her feelings of disappointment were related to the knowledge that her own mother wished to spend this time with her grandchildren and also how typical grandparent support seemed to be in Korea. While she was living in Australia her mother had regularly traveled an hour on weekends to see her granddaughter in order to maintain a relationship despite distance and work commitments.

> I feel a bit sorry for my mum. . . but a little bit, a little bit sad that I can't get, you know, a little bit more support from my mother-in-law which I sort of thought that I might be able to because it sort of seems kind of, very, very common here. (Sue)

Sue described how modifying her expectations had been an important part of how she managed this disappointment after realizing that the amount of support she had hoped to receive from her mother-in-law wasn't in line with what she was prepared to offer. She had subsequently found alternative ways to foster the relationship between her children and their Korean grandmother. This included being available for important family functions even if her husband wasn't, regularly visiting her in-laws with the children or alternatively encouraging the children to call them.

Jamie also felt that she would have more family support if she returned to America. Like Sue, she also lived a short distance from her in-laws and knew she could rely on either her parents-in-law or sister-in-law to help out with her daughter if her work commitments kept her from making it to day care on time. She also commented, however, that because her mother-in-law is older she is very hands-off.

> She's not the nightmare mother-in-law I hear at all. Um, she has
> her opinions but she keeps them mostly to herself. (Jamie)

She appeared to be evaluating her mother-in-law against the negative stereotypes she envisioned in the descriptions of other women's experiences.

Jamie's situation was also complicated by her mother's health concerns and a desire to be near her mother during this time. Similarly to Sue, Jamie felt that both of her parents would be more involved in the lives of her children were she to return to America. She described how her parents, particularly her mother, were more vocal about their opinions in raising her daughters than her mother-in-law is. She struggled with her mother's requests for her family to return knowing it isn't financially viable. This was exasperated by her mother's cancer treatment. Sue's and Jamie's experiences demonstrate that when assessing acculturation and needs of an Anglophone woman in Korea, traditional expectations of family support cannot necessarily be assumed. It also reflects the burden they can potentially feel toward their families of origin which can be intensified by distance.

In their responses, many of the women described how they were trying to include their in-laws in holidays and traditions which were significant to them. As previously demonstrated in the discussion of how the participants were utilizing social media in order to coordinate and celebrate holidays, finding ways to observe these holidays was important to these women. Dianne's flexible approach to celebrating American holidays had also expanded to the way she celebrated with her in-laws. The Christmas before the interview, when her parents in America had asked what presents to prepare for Christmas, she had asked them to buy a catered turkey meal which is now available in Korea, in lieu of presents. Her rationale behind this choice was a combination of wanting to share the holidays with her inlaws and also wanting to limit the amount of toys for her children due to limited space in their home.

Jamie described the challenges she faced in her efforts to include her family-in-law in her traditions. There were certain cultural barriers which had emerged when she had previously invited them to share the Thanksgiving meals she had prepared. One year her sister-in-law had brought crab to share as a gesture of gratitude. This had resulted in the majority of her turkey dinner and trimmings being left uneaten and the lengthy preparation wasted. A second year when she had invited them, she had tried to initiate a discussion about which food was the favorite, which she described as a normal post-Thanksgiving dinner discussion. This had been met with blanket replies from her in-laws claiming that they had enjoyed all the dishes in order to be polite. She was aware that they had not wanted to offend her, being conscious of the fact that she had prepared the food by herself. She contrasted this with the enjoyment and ease of another Thanksgiving celebration when she had only invited her expatriate friends to celebrate.

Jamie expressed a desire to have a combined celebration with her American friends and her in-laws. Her hope was that in allowing her in-laws to experience a celebration with her American friends, they would be able to begin to learn and understand the significance and meaning behind the holidays more easily. Her husband, however, did not support this proposal. Jamie's responses show how the women were actively trying to integrate not only their cultures but their social circles.

Charlotte's responses further illustrate the important role the husband played in the celebration of holidays. Whereas Dianne alluded to the potential for disappointment when seeking to recreate childhood memories around important holidays, it was these kinds of disappointments which had prompted a serious discussion between Charlotte and her husband. They took the time to discuss the expectations surrounding various holidays and outlined a detailed plan of how their family would observe each of the holidays in a way that everyone was satisfied with. This list included Christmas, Easter, birthdays, and also their anniversary. It was a formal plan that even described the kinds of gifts which would be given.

Although none of the other women described how they had formally planned the celebration of holidays to this detail, many of them had some form of arrangement or were in the process of negotiating acceptable ways to observe their traditions. Contrary to the discussions of assimilation which is often assumed and facilitated in many of the policies regarding multiculturalism in Korea, highlighted in previous chapters, it appears that the women were hopeful for much more of a cultural exchange. However, their responses demonstrate that the level to which this was true and the level of integration they hoped for did in fact vary for each individual in a way which would be suggested by the principle of specificity in acculturation already introduced.

5.5 Korean Support Systems

5.5.1 Children's Carers and Educators

The Korean carers and education providers of the women's children emerged as an important part of their parenting experience. Although education was discussed to some extent in terms of the impact the mother's level of Korean fluency had on communication with teachers, it also had wider implications in terms of a support network for the mother. Aside from Nicky who had yet to place her child in the Korean education system, all of the women described positive experiences with their children's schooling. Andrea had described it as a really positive transition for both her sons. Justine expressed gratitude for the care, gentleness, and patience she had seen the teachers show her son in the four different centers he had attended. Their experiences also demonstrated the extent to which the Korean teachers went to bridge the cultural divide for the mother. This was particularly demonstrated in the responses of Jessica, Maggie, and Dianne.

Whereas the language barrier with their children's teachers impacted and concerned the mothers to different extents, some of the interviewees described how their children's teachers were actively trying to bridge that gap. Jessica's daughter's teacher had even gone to the extent of utilizing a translation application on her phone in order for her to be able to exchange messages with her in English. This had been particularly comforting when her daughter had first started kindergarten and had been struggling with the transition. She gave examples of the awkward translations in some of the messages, but it was clear that it was secondary to the fact that through the effort the teacher extended, Jessica recognized the care that it represented.

Maggie described the support from her son's government combined day care/kindergarten as meeting her halfway. She recognized this as a positive impact of the multicultural family guidelines and training her son's teachers had received. Her son had been attending the same center for four years after a less positive experience in her previous day care, one that will be discussed in the next chapter. In her interview she described how she found that part of the exhaustion and mental load from the effort of raising her child bilingual and multicultural had been somewhat alleviated by the willingness of her son's school to recognize her need for additional support and also aid in integration. Her son's teachers used various strategies to support her, such as using basic Korean, and making sure her son reiterated in English what had been communicated in order to make sure important information about upcoming events would not be missed. In addition to the interviews, she sent pictures of her giving a lesson to the children at her son's school for a special "Canadian Day" where she taught about Halloween, a holiday that holds special significance to her.

Maggie's experience illustrates a very practical method which is already being implemented by early childhood educators in Korea. It also highlights the importance of their role in providing a multicultural narrative which goes beyond assimilation and facilitates awareness and the normalizing of multicultural families in Korean society. Furthermore, in conducting a support network assessment of marriage immigrants, a pastoral caregiver can assess the level of openness and support the mother is receiving from her child's education center as a potential asset to their care.

5.5.2 Husbands and Korean Friends

Alongside the support from teachers, the mothers in the study also described how their husbands and even other Korean mothers had become important channels of support in terms of their child's education. Although Jessica had expressed how important it was for her to navigate life in Korea, including her children's education, independently of her Korean husband, many of the mothers described the support their husbands provided. Maggie, Francis, and Dianne all described the role their husbands had played in communicating, especially in regard to reading and writing important information in their child's school communication book as well as other information and notices sent from the school. Francis's husband had initially expected her to handle all of the communication herself but after some fighting, had realized that it was too much for her to manage while she was also working full time.

While actively trying to improve and manage the communication with her children's day care, Dianne also described the support her husband offered. Being a teacher himself, Dianne's husband had reassured her that as their children progressed through the Korean education system that he would be able to assist with the additional duties and responsibilities requested from parents by Korean schools. She had however considered the potential impact of these dynamics. Her husband had recently been talking with a student of his who had an American father and a Korean mother. Although she was comforted to hear how well adjusted the student was, she also pondered how much of this was a result of having a Korean mother to navigate the education system rather than a father. Dianne's observations illustrate her awareness of how gender roles and norms in Korean society have the potential to impact the educational experience of diverse multi-cultural families living in Korea in different ways.

Along with support from her husband, Francis had also benefited from the help of Korean mothers in her son's school. As her children progressed through the Korean education system, Francis appeared to rely less on the support of the expatriate community and more on other Korean mothers.

> Korean moms have been really nice to me. In, in helping me, like they always give me information. They've never been rude to me when I've asked like what's going on. (Francis)

When her son had entered into his first year of elementary school the mother of one of his friends had requested that their children be placed in the same class so that she would be able to help her navigate the change. Similarly, Justine commented on how when she had moved into her new neighborhood the mothers from her son's day care had approached her in the playground on the first day. Given her general lack of support from her in-laws, this reassured her and gave her a sense that perhaps she could begin to draw on that support network if necessary.

Justine and Charlotte described how the after-school programs had also provided their children with a sense of community. Both of them described how the experience of sending their children to an after-school academy to learn the traditional Korean martial art *Taekwondo* had led to their children developing relationships with older children. Justine observed and appreciated how as a part of Korean culture the older children were taught to take care of the younger children in a way which she felt doesn't happen in Canada. This care which the older children showed toward the younger children, particularly through the academy, was one of the factors which Charlotte also recognized and felt afforded her children the opportunity to be more independent in Korea.

Charlotte told of how the older children in her son's *Taekwondo* academy also look out for her son on the school playground and remind him to attend his various after-school activities. She even gave an example of how recently she had utilized this community, asking these children where they had last seen her son when he hadn't shown up to his *Taekwondo* class. For her, this community of children afforded by the after-school academies not only facilitated this growing independence, but she felt that in Korea it was also more socially acceptable to allow your children the freedom to navigate around to different activities without a guardian from an earlier age than in Canada. This was highlighted to her by the concerns raised by her mother when her eldest son had visited Canada by himself two years previously.

The discussions Charlotte had with her mother while her son had been staying in Canada without her illustrated for her the amount of freedom and independence afforded to children at a younger age in Korea. She described many discussions with her mother to highlight the differences. Her son had been surprised by how much his maternal grandmother had emphasized that he needed to stay together with her at all times. Charlotte's mother had been concerned that her grandson had failed to learn her name and contact details in case he went missing. These conversations had caused Charlotte to feel a huge change in her mother from when she was a child. Growing up, Sarah's mother had been a single parent and as the eldest, Sarah had been responsible for walking her younger siblings to school.

> I just thought it was what I saw on the media until my son actually went there and I went there and I realized how grateful I am to be raising my children in Korea, where they are not scared of strangers and they're not scared to be alone and they're willing to go out and play and have fun and have adventures still. (Charlotte)

So, for Charlotte, the sense of community that after-school programs such as *Taekwondo* fostered for her children allowed her to give them a similar sense of freedom and independence that she remembers from her childhood in a way that the current Canadian society wouldn't necessary allow for. It also represents different understandings that sometimes occur between the immigrant mother and her mother in her country of origin.

5.6 Connections with Mothers in the Motherland

Charlotte's description of her first trip home also highlighted differences of experience and opinions that some of the participants had with their mothers. During her first visit to Canada with her eldest son her mother had questioned her about her son's routine, napping habits, and discomfort with a car seat. Particularly in relation to the car seat and her son napping in a carrier, her choices had been largely shaped by her Korean context where she predominantly walked everywhere, but they had also been shaped by a lack of awareness of these Canadian parenting norms and taboos.

Similarly, whereas Jamie described her mother-in-law as relatively hands off, her mother was more vocal in her input in a way that didn't always fully grasp her daughter's context. She told how her own mother had criticized her choice to keep her daughter in day care for extended hours. Jamie's mother had contrasted this with the way she had raised her. Furthermore, Jamie also described how her mother's requests for her and her family to relocate back to America failed to recognize not only the ties she had to her host country but also the complicated process of applying for and obtaining her husband's American visa. To a lesser extent, Nicky also described the differences in parenting philosophies she held with her own mother surrounding spanking. This is also what led her to conclude that even differences with her parents-in-law were perhaps generational in as much as they were cultural.

Rather than highlighting the differences she held with her mother, Maggie's responses described how raising her child as an expatriate in Korea meant that she had to consider a variety of different factors which her mother hadn't. When discussing her decisions regarding exposing her son to different traditions in relation to religion, holidays, language, and even food, she was aware that her mother did not have to negotiate these things to the same extent.

> So those things are all intentional. It's always something that I'm thinking about or I have put a lot of thought into that's now easier now that he's six and I'm used to it, it's like my new normal sort of thing. But those aren't things that my mother thought about. (Maggie)

These responses of the participants demonstrate how they were actively processing and negotiating how their parenting context and experience differed from their own mothers.

5.7 The Communal Aspect of Raising Children in Korea

Community was both needed and experienced by the women in various ways. As demonstrated in the previous sections, Facebook and the internet more generally facilitated their connections both to the community in Korea and with family and friends in their country of origin. Many of the women also expressed how the communal aspect of Korean culture had added another aspect of community in a way which was both positive and negative.

Sue especially described how motherhood in Korea had become a more communal experience than it would have been back in Australia. Like many of the other participants, she described how this was both positive and negative. She described how she had at times felt quite pressured when difficult parenting moments emerged in public spaces and people had tried to intervene or give suggestions. However, she also reasoned that this was probably reflective of their willingness to help.

> I reasoned that if people are actually willing to approach you on the street then they're probably also willing to help. (Sue)

> I also felt like I can lean on people more, that I can ask for help or that I can expect help from people whereas I didn't feel that in Australia. (Sue)

This was elaborated on through the example provided of an experience she recalled illustrating what parenting in Korea meant for her. Throughout the interview Sue had struggled to recollect one incident which she felt embodied her motherhood experience in Korea. As a result, she contacted the researcher after the interview with a written description of what she later recalled and chose as representative. She described how she had been stuck alone in public with her daughter who had unexpectedly soiled her pants. A middle-aged woman who had been in a store nearby not only noticed her predicament, but promptly met her with half a packet of wet wipe tissues explaining that she didn't need the remainder back. Just as quickly as she appeared, she left and then after a few moments sent her son out to give Sue a plastic bag.

Justine also described how she had benefited from the support of passing strangers. This had been both positive and negative from her perspective. She illustrated her point with examples of both instances. She also described how she had come to think of the communal aspects of parenting more positively over time whereas her husband had come to be more troubled by the perceived intrusions. Justine had a home birth with her first son and brought him to the hospital at two days old. During the hospital visit she had been confronted with an older Korean woman pulling back the cloth wrap carrier she was using to hold her newborn in order to gain a closer look at him. She understood the Korean notion of "our baby" which she reasoned had most likely caused the woman to feel that this behavior was completely appropriate and not overstepping the boundaries of over-familiarity for a stranger.[1] Even so, she had felt it was very intrusive. As a result, she had responded in a way which had caused an argument between her and her husband.

Justine gave a second illustration which also described the ways she had come to see this interest in her child as advantageous. She recounted an incident where her son was refusing to continue to walk to their home. Seeing this, an elderly Korean man had subsequently walked down the hill, took her son's hand and walked back up the hill together with them. These day-to-day interactions where the mothers began to realize they were able to draw on the support of Korean society in general also developed through the responses of the participants into a deeper theme of acceptance of Korean society for both the mother and the child and will be covered in the next chapter.

---

1. Korean culture and a sense of community are embedded in the language. In the Korean language you would not refer to an infant, toddler, or child as "My" baby or so forth. The appropriate pronoun is *woori* (우리) which translates into English as "our." Hence, the child literally becomes "our baby," not "yours" or "mine."

Chapter 6

NURTURE:
The Cultural and Social Identity
of the Mother and Child

ANOTHER IMPORTANT THEME WHICH emerged from the participant's responses was that of *Cultural and Social Identity*, not in terms of identity formation but more in terms of acceptance into Korean society. This generally fell into two categories: the acceptance of the mother into Korean society and the acceptance of their child. In general, the mothers expressed more passionate responses in relation to the acceptance of their children into Korean society as it reflected a desire that almost all of them had for their children to have a strong connection with their Korean identity and culture. Many of them told of playground episodes in various detail describing the attention their children and they themselves received in the playground. Even though the playground was a powerful setting for this negotiation of acceptance and Korean identity, the attention was not limited to incidents occurring there. The attention they and their children received contributed to the sense of being outsiders. Given that the Korean word for foreigner *Waegukin* can be literally translated as "outside one" or "one who is outside" it is not surprising that many of the women had particularly emotive responses to their children being addressed in this way.

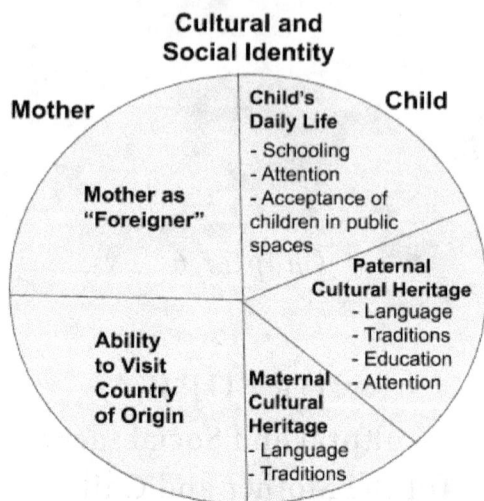

Diagram 3: Cultural and Social Identity

6.1 Mother as Foreigner

Some of the women such as Justine had become so accustomed to the attention specifically related to being a foreigner in Korea, that it no longer bothered them. Nicky even described how she was often only reminded of being different when she heard Koreans speaking to her son in English and their surprised reaction when he could understand Korean. Maggie's responses, however, described a deeper acceptance into Korean society which she felt would always be unobtainable for her.

> I am for all intents and purposes an immigrant, but I am seen as an expat and it's pretty impossible for me to become Korean. Even if I, if we, even if I literally became Korean, I'll never really be Korean in other people's eyes. (Maggie)

Although she recognized that in some ways this afforded her and her son some leeway if they failed to adhere to societal norms in public, she also described how this impacted her experience in raising her son in more complicated ways.

Maggie described many times her son's capacity and even development had been called into question and any failings were attributed to her "foreignness." As described in the previous chapter, Maggie's experience at her son's current school had been very positive but she also recalled subtle messages from her son's first day care which were more negative. She remembered the teachers attributing her son's failure to eat certain side dishes to her being a foreigner. This sentiment was reflected in comments such as "You must not like mushrooms because your mom is a foreigner." Furthermore, she found that when she was with her son and he spoke Korean, people had at times refused to accept the fact that he could speak Korean because his mother was a foreigner. She recalled people telling her son he was speaking English when he was actually speaking Korean. When her husband had corrected them, they had told him,

> "Oh, well that's . . . you're not really speaking Korean because your mom's a foreigner. Unless you're speaking it with an English accent." (Maggie)

Maggie noted that as her son had grown older some of that tension had been alleviated as he was able to start advocating for his multicultural identity for himself. She was, however, aware of how her presence did create complications for her son being accepted as a typical Korean. Although a number of the mothers had expressed how their children visibly looked non-Korean, Maggie was the only participant to comment on how if her son was not with her, he would not necessarily be perceived as a biracial child. She described how if he was out with her husband without her, they would usually be perceived as a typical Korean father and son.

Sue also expressed similar challenges to Maggie in how she had seen her competency as a parent attributed to her foreignness.

> Sometimes I get a sense sometimes there is a perception that it's my foreignness that makes me incompetent to other people. (Sue)

Sue saw the advantages of Korea's communal culture when out in public and appreciated how she was able to lean on others for help as mentioned in the previous chapter about community. Even so, she also admitted to feeling frustrated by the tendency for this attention to turn into unwarranted public instruction. Despite feeling frustrated by these encounters, Sue was intentional in simply accepting the advice in the moment rather than arguing. This was due to a lack of willingness to enhance a bad perception of foreigners through actions which could be perceived as aggressive, which she felt was particularly necessary if she was dealing with people who already thought she was incompetent on the basis that she was a foreigner to them.

Although many of the mothers were not particularly concerned with receiving attention for their foreignness per se, some did express how they felt that due to the attention they received, their motherhood was on display in some respects. Maggie felt that because she was more recognizable and noticeable when she was out in public, she often felt slightly paranoid. Because she was not only being watched but noticeable as a foreigner, she felt like her motherhood was somehow on display and she was representing all foreign mothers. It created a burden for her as she was concerned that other's observations of her would form the basis of their opinions of other foreign mothers more generally. Even so, she was aware that despite feeling this way, it may not necessarily be the case. She also knew that similar things happened in Canada where people would generalize about someone from a different country or culture based on a small number of interactions with one or two people with that background. However, she also perceived the lack of diversity in Korea as exasperating the situation.

Justine also wished at times that when she was out in public that she was less noticeable. Although in general the additional attention didn't concern her, there were times that it did. Given that children and mothers would often come up to her and her son when they were in children's cafes, she couldn't just leisurely observe her son at play the way she noticed other Korean mothers do.

Other mothers understood the attention they received in different ways. Nicky and Charlotte described how they were often unaware of the attention they received. Sue's response also reflected that the attention in and of itself did not contribute to her feeling selfconscious, even if she at times felt like her competence was being evaluated on the basis of being a foreigner.

> I'm not conscious of, of people looking at me. I don't really care too much about how people, you know, whether people pay attention to me or whatever. (Sue)

As will be elaborated in the following sections, she was more concerned with the affect the additional attention was having on her daughter.

Sue and Maggie both felt that Korea has a culture that is more accepting of children than their country of origin. Maggie felt that there were very few places in Korea where it would be inappropriate to bring a child. In contrast, she regularly returned to Canada with her son for extended periods over the summer and even though she recognized things were changing, she had often felt disapproving looks from people when she had tried to bring her son to places which were not specifically marketed towards children and families. Sue also noted that there were a wide range of places which tailored to children in Korea but also that there was more tolerance for children in public spaces more generally.

> Like if I'm in a cafe or something, I don't feel like everybody's star-
> ing at me like thinking, "Oh my God, she brought a child, hehehe,
> with her" but I definitely had those kinds of experiences a lot in
> Australia of just feeling people's judgment. (Sue)

Maggie and Sue recognized the acceptance of children in Korean public spaces in general. The previous chapter also demonstrated how this often extended to a sense of communal parenting which had its advantages and drawbacks. There was a general sense that children were welcomed in public spaces but many of the participants described the struggle to have their child accepted as Korean citizens.

6.2 Korean Identity of the Child

The theme of acceptance in relation to the child also reflects the importance the mother placed on their child's multicultural identity. In many of the descriptions of the kind of attention their children received, the tension for many was the desire for their children to be recognized and accepted as Korean citizens. For the mothers, this was one important element of their child's identity. In their responses, all of the women, except Sue, expressed the importance they placed on their child having a firm grasp of the cultures of both of their parents. It doesn't however follow that their child's cultural identity was limited to the cultures of their parents. This is seen particularly in relation to Maggie and Francis intentionally referring to their children as multicultural rather than bicultural. Despite Korea's identification as a homogeneous society, for them Korea afforded them many opportunities to foster their child's multicultural identity.

Maggie was especially purposeful in exposing her son to different cultures and educating him about them. She saw herself juggling three cultures in the home and also recognized that by living in Korea her son was exposed to other cultures and people through the expatriate community. Alongside Korean and Canadian culture, which she understood as being very multifaceted, Maggie also saw herself juggling religion as a third culture in their home. Furthermore, Maggie saw that the same dynamic which kept her from being accepted as a Korean also contributed to other expatriates maintaining more of their cultural identity from their country of origin. Whereas in Canada their country of origin's cultural identity would become one aspect of their Canadian identity, she saw it as remaining more distinct in Korea. This afforded her son the opportunity to become exposed to different cultures.

Exposing her children to different cultural experiences was an advantage Francis attributed to raising her children in Korea, albeit in a slightly different way to Maggie. Given the proximity of Korea to other countries in Asia specifically, living in Korea allowed her family more opportunities to travel and see different cultures firsthand. She described how if she were living with her family in Canada, she would most likely only travel to Mexico or America. While living in Korea she had not only been able to take her children back to Canada four times, but also to Taiwan. Similarly, Nicky listed being able to travel with her son and introduce him to other cultures as an advantage.

Just as the Korean education system alongside the teachers and parents provided an important support system for the mothers, they also valued the multicultural opportunities it provided. In a similar way to how Maggie had been invited into her son's kindergarten to give a Canadian culture lesson where she had taught on Halloween, the elementary school where Charlotte's children attended also exposed them to other cultures.

> They have multicultural programs where they had different teachers, a Vietnamese teacher come in, a Chinese teacher come in, a Japanese teacher come in, with traditional dress and game and language, and I was really surprised that they had the benefit of getting to try other cultures in their elementary school. (Charlotte)

As discussed in the first chapter, Chinese and Vietnamese women represent the highest percentage of spouses in international marriages in Korea. Subsequently, these lessons her children had were most likely a result of a Korean government multicultural initiative. Charlotte for one, had not only experienced this program but viewed it very positively.

For many of the participants in the study the Korean education system also played a crucial part in educating their children in Korean culture. Integration of her son's cultural identities was an important priority for Maggie. Her intentionality in her cultural and linguistic efforts was for the purpose of providing a foundation in which her son could develop a healthy, integrated sense of identity and self. She described how she had observed her son effortlessly blending and flowing between language and culture and she acknowledged the way his Korean education had contributed to that.

> I could not have the son that I have without the Korean education system. (Maggie)

She was aware of the limitations to her ability to teach her son Korean culture and how having him treated as a normal Korean person in his school allowed him to develop that part of his identity.

Dianne's experience with day care was also an important avenue for the development of her daughter's Korean identity which she saw very positively. She described day care as her daughter's own private Korean world which was reinforced through the center's use of her Korean name. Unlike some of her friends who only wanted their children to have one name, Dianne and her husband had given their children two names. At day care her daughter is known by her Korean name whereas at home Dianne calls her by her English name. This helped her come to accept the fact that although she saw both of her children as American, they were also Korean and being raised in Korea.

Francis also appreciated the cultural aspect of her children's education which she saw beginning from day care. While valuing the various cultural experiences afforded by living in Korea, she appreciated the etiquette classes her children had participated in which had taught her sons how to wear their Korean traditional outfits and bow appropriately as part of the Korean holiday customs. She wanted them to feel proud of their Korean culture.

The sentiment of wanting their children to be proud of their Korean heritage and its link to the observation of Korean holiday traditions was indicated in the responses of almost all the participants. Alongside the description of how their families celebrated holidays from their cultural traditions, the women described how they observed Korean holidays, especially the Korean Thanksgiving and Lunar New Year holidays, with the Korean side of their family. A number of the participants besides Sue, whose in-laws and husband seemed somewhat more traditional by comparison, described how these holidays were generally more laid back when compared to their knowledge of the customs usually practiced around the holidays which are generally understood to be particularly burdensome on the women of the family.

Many described how their families no longer prepared the *Jesa* tables filled with food usually made around the two major Korean holidays. *Jesa* is traditionally observed with male family members bowing before tables filled with food usually prepared by the women of the family in order to honor family members who have passed away. Many of the participants, especially those with Christian in-laws, told how their families no longer observed this particular tradition. Nicky described how she wasn't expected to participate in the food preparation around the holidays given that her husband's family already had a large number of women who were willing to contribute. Unlike Nicky, Jamie did participate in the food preparation.

Although Jamie's family did not participate in *Jesa*, food preparation had been a part of her participation in the Korean holidays early in her marriage. However, the focus of the holidays had shifted after having children. Her husband's family did not celebrate with large gatherings of extended family, but they did follow other traditions. Using the example of the Lunar New Year holiday, she shared how they were teaching their daughter to participate in the tradition of bowing to her grandparents and receiving money.

> You know, now it's, it's about teaching my daughters this, this side of their heritage. (Jamie)

The holidays had become less about her learning the traditions of the Korean holidays and more about teaching them to her daughters.

In total, the participant's responses surrounding their family's observations of Korean holiday traditions demonstrated that they were aware of and respectful of the traditions and the accompanying obligations they held, particularly for women in the family. More important to them, however, was how observing these holidays reflected their desire for their children to be exposed to and engaged in their Korean cultural heritage.

Beyond celebrating the Korean holidays, Charlotte's responses also highlight the emphasis she placed on her children's Korean cultural identity formation. Many of Charlotte's responses reflected a narrative of her goal in raising "good Korean citizens," which was a phrase she repeated a number of times throughout the interview. This was not at the expense of their Canadian identity, but due to their context of living in Korea.

> I often don't think about raising my children as multiracial. I'm trying to raise them as good Koreans. Canadians second. (Charlotte)

> For the most part we live as a Korean family first and Canadian
> family second . . . Just because we are in Korea and we want our
> children to have a strong grasp of Korean culture, language, and
> identity. (Charlotte)

In practice, this meant that although English is the dominant language
in the home, they eat predominately Korean food, and importance is placed
on teaching Korean traditions and culture. It was due to this effort that she
is offended when people call her children nonKorean.

The playground was often, although not exclusively, the setting where
the mothers and their children drew attention both due to their appearance
and to their use of language. Many of the women described having strong
reactions to the attention they and their children received, especially when
their child's Korean identity was ignored and they were labeled as being
foreigners.

Jessica distinguished the reactions she and her children received in
public into three categories. Firstly, she described some reactions as simply
indifferent. The second group of people were those who would give her
children praise based on their different appearance. Some had even gone so
far as to try and take pictures with her children or even kiss them, although
it more commonly involved touch. Finally, there were the people who she
felt were really bothered by the presence of her and her children. Of the
three categories she felt like the second and third were the majority.

Her description of the final category of people also demonstrated her
knowledge of the narrative of Korean homogeneity.

> My feeling is that they really hate you . . . because you have the
> nerve to like, you know, procreate with a Korean and you know,
> tarnish the pure Korean bloodline. (Jessica)

Experiencing mostly encounters with the second and third categories
of people had caused her to develop anxiety about going outside. This was
contrary to her usually outgoing personality and how she envisioned raising her children in America.

Although Jessica was the only one to describe the attention she received as either hostile or indifferent, many of the participants detailed the
attention their children received on the basis of being different or on their
use of language. Many mentioned that this attention could either be positive or negative and it bothered the women to various degrees. Like Jessica,
Justine, Jamie, and Andrea discussed having their children's appearance

praised in various ways. They were told that their children were beautiful, gorgeous, pretty, cute, and even that they looked like a doll. Koreans would also often comment on their children's eyes. Many of the women simply described this as positive attention and didn't really appear to be bothered by it at all. Jessica however raised concerns about the nature of some of the praise.

Jessica had some reservations about even some of the well-intended attention her daughter received. She told of incidents when people were admiring her daughter's large eyes and would comment that it was fortunate that she wouldn't have to pay to have eyelid surgery later. She admitted that this was preferable to the more hostile encounters, but she held concerns for her daughter's sense of self-worth.

> I don't want her to have her only like, self-identity of being about her looks. (Jessica)

Aside from appearance, the children often drew attention in public for speaking English, particularly on the playground. This form of attention was much more closely related to acceptance. Charlotte and Nicky both described how the multiracial aspect of their family was often only brought to the forefront of their attention when they were out in public and English suddenly became emphasized. For Nicky, this was when people would approach her son speaking English and then express surprise that he was able to speak and understand Korean. Charlotte's family received attention in public not just due to their appearance, but also due to using English as a first language as a family. She felt like the only time the multiracial aspect of her motherhood was drawn to her attention was when they were out in public and people would call them *waegukin* or foreigner. Reflecting on the emphasis she had placed on raising her children to be accepted as Koreans, she would often correct them and tell them that they were Koreans.

Francis's response expressed the irony that her children were still called foreigners on the very playground they had been playing in their whole lives.

> Sometimes you'll still get somebody pointing and saying waegukin so [trails off before restarting] You're the stranger here. Hahaha. But, we live here. Who are you? (Francis)

Although at first Francis would ask them to stop by explaining it wasn't very nice, she and her sons would often just ignore it unless the comments were more serious. She reasoned that they were simply being children.

Sue also had experiences of her daughter being approached on the playground. Despite her daughter being more fluent and comfortable communicating in Korean, Sue often observed parents encouraging their children to approach her daughter in English.

> She doesn't really speak a lot of English. But, but even if she did, you know, there's a sense that she's not people's English teacher and she's not um, she's not foreign. She's, she's kind of foreign, but she's Korean. (Sue)

Again, Sue's response reflects the desire of many of the participants for their child's Korean identity to be accepted. She described this as navigating her daughter's perceived foreignness.

Like the other mothers, although Sue was accustomed to the regular attention, she was more aware of it from her daughter's perspective. She recognized how overwhelmed her daughter became when they initially moved into their current residence and people had repeatedly called out "foreigner" after seeing her daughter play. As mentioned previously, Sue saw her Korean proficiency as playing an important role in helping to diminish her daughter's perceived foreignness. It not only helped her to be aware of what was causing her daughter to feel overwhelmed but it also taught her to advocate for herself by being able to learn appropriate ways of responding in these kinds of situations.

Like Francis, Justine would prefer to simply ignore the attention unless she felt it was necessary to address. She recognized that when she was out with her husband and son, a lot of the attention was curiosity, particularly at their use of language. Whereas Justine had grown accustomed to the attention directed at her after ten years of living in Korea, her husband had grown gradually more bothered by it, particularly after the birth of their son. For his part, her son had already started to recognize how he was able to use his Korean proficiency to charm Koreans, particularly the older generation.

Justine, however, also recounted one less positive incident on the playground with a child who was particularly insistent on drawing attention to the fact that she appeared to be able to speak English. His insistence was despite the fact that she had been playing with her son and the other children using Korean. Understanding that children and adults were often just curious, her family most typically chose to simply walk away from these kinds of situations. On this occasion, however, the child had continued to return to Justine and her son while repeatedly pointing out to the others they were playing with that they were "English people." It was less the words than the child's insistence which were problematic for Justine. This was particularly so when he started to approach other children telling them to speak to her in English despite the fact that she had been interacting with them in Korean up until that point.

As mentioned previously, Jessica had described how various kinds of negative attention she received in public with her children had contributed to her developing anxiety. She also described a playground incident related to her speaking English with her daughter which had caused her to stop going to the playground for a period of time. Her daughter who hadn't attended kindergarten at that point wasn't able to understand what the older girls were saying to them. Jessica, however, understood that they were laughing and pointing at them for communicating in English. This had left her feeling terrible because after that incident she was mostly keeping her daughter at home rather than giving her the kind of experiences she would if they were living in America.

6.3 Bilingualism

All of the mothers in the survey highlighted their children's bilingualism as an advantage to them being raised in Korea. They were all in agreement that if the children were to be raised in their mother's country of origin it would not only be more difficult for the children to learn Korean cultural and social norms, but language as well.

> If my child were raised in Canada it would be much harder for him to learn the Korean language and that, it would be extremely hard for him to learn Korean social norms and engagement norms. (Maggie)

> I think it would be a struggle for my kids to be bilingual if we lived in, in California. Because I grew up with a lot of Asian Americans but um, um even the ones who were bilingual, I mean they couldn't necessarily read or write well in their, ah in the minority language. (Dianne)

Because Nicky had not yet sent her son to school, she recognized bilingualism as being a part of her motherhood experience in Korea. This was for the practical reason of raising her son bilingual in order for him to communicate with both sides of his family. Similarly, Maggie's responses indicate the importance the women placed on language for relational connection.

Maggie expressed clearly articulated ideals and strategies for her son's development both culturally and linguistically. Although her husband hadn't considered these issues in the same detail, Maggie was aware he still had priorities for his son which included language.

> I think I, because I am very strong in caring about my culture and my language and making it at the forefront, my husband goes along with that because I'm a stronger personality than he is in that. But at the same time, he wants to be able to speak his own language to his child. And he wants his child to succeed academically. (Maggie)

Although her husband wanted to be able to speak Korean with his son, Maggie noted how it was an adjustment for him at first given that prior to the birth of their son, their home had been a predominately English environment. This demonstrates that there was an understanding, even if not particularly articulated, between Maggie and her husband as to the importance language and culture played in the life of their child.

Whereas many of the mothers, such as Andrea and Nicky, described how people would often express surprise at their child's ability to speak Korean, Justine's responses went into deeper reflection on their reactions. Justine had experienced people being very concerned about the challenges that could be caused by raising their child bilingual. Her mother-in-law and son's previous day care teachers had expressed concerns over whether her son would be able to understand and be confident in both languages. Given her experience studying in a French immersion school as a child and her study in linguistics, Justine did not have these concerns. She drew on her experiential and educational background to reassure them that there was little cause for these concerns. She understood that the concerns these people were raising were based on Korea having, for the most part, a very unilingual history. From her understanding, only one generation ago it was very unusual to be raised with two languages in Korea. Whereas others were concerned with if her son was able to process both languages, for Justine it was simply the normal he was being raised with.

Andrea's responses also reflected sensitivity to the perception that her son would struggle with both languages. During the interview she had assumed a follow-up question about her experience with day care was only asking for negative experiences. This was revealed through the researcher probing deeper into her responses that her experiences with day care had all been positive. Through reflection she realized she had responded this way because she was aware that there is a perception that being a multicultural family and bilingual more specifically, would present difficulties for herself and her son. She was aware that some may think that her son would find it difficult to move from an English environment at home to a Korean environment at day care, which hadn't been the case.

> . . . because most of the times we think about multicultural we think that it's so hard and that we are gonna have many negative experiences. (Andrea)

> I guess when I think of it as multicultural and you asked me how is day care, I think that oh, maybe it's gonna be harder for him in day care, be more negative because he, suddenly it's another language. (Andrea)

Just as Justine's background informed her approach to her son's bilingualism, Francis's Masters in Teaching English as a Second Language also informed her linguistic decisions. Francis intentionally only engaged with her sons in English in order to raise her children bilingual. Whereas the majority of her parenting decisions were made on the basis of what worked for her and her family, her use of English with her sons was heavily informed by her education, in a similar way to Justine. This demonstrates the intentionality the women demonstrated in approaching the language acquisition of her children. Through Francis's responses it also became clear that she valued visiting Canada for how these trips also contributed to her sons' bilingualism. She illustrated this through contrasting her experience with that of another Anglophone friend who is also married to a Korean.

Francis contrasted her experience with her New Zealand friend whose Korean-New Zealand children refuse to speak to her in English. This contrast was expressed in a way which indicated that her son's bilingual success was somewhat attributed to her strategies. She described how in contrast to her friend, she did not allow her children to speak Korean to her. Furthermore, she described how her sons had been able to travel to Canada four times whereas her friend's children had never been to New Zealand. This demonstrates a further function that visiting their country of origin served for these women aside from facilitating relationships between their children and family of origin as mentioned in the previous chapters.

The bilingual exposure her son received was perceived as advantageous, however, as he grew older, Maggie recognized her son responding in interesting ways to demands placed on his language proficiency. Maggie told of incidents she had experienced in both Canada and Korea where out of curiosity people would demand her son perform either English or Korean. She explained how in Korea people would on occasion demand that her son speak English to them and in Canada people would demand that he speak to them in Korean. She emphasized that it was never a gentle request but a demand to perform language which her normally outgoing son refused to accommodate.

Even though their sons were around four years younger than Maggie's, Andrea and Justine also recognized their child's ability to identify appropriate times to use Korean rather than English. Both Justine and Andrea's sons were around three years old at the time of the study. Even at this age, Justine told how when Korean people approached her son in English, he would speak to them in Korean and not in English because he recognized that they were Korean. Similarly, Andrea shared how her three-year-old son had no difficulty switching between languages. Her recollection of a playground incident in which her son had spoken to some Korean children in English rather than in Korean was raised for the reason that it was unusual behavior for him.

These illustrations demonstrate that the mothers were aware of the advantages of raising their children bilingual and many were actively trying to do so. They saw it functioning in various ways in their children's lives. It was necessary for them to communicate with both sides of their families, an important part of their cultural identity, and also something they necessarily navigated in their interactions in Korean society, particularly in the playground.

6.4 Teaching Traditions from Home

Alongside acceptance of their child's Korean identity, the participants also discussed how important it was for them to pass on their own cultural traditions. As has been described previously, this was particularly evident to various extents for many of the participants in the ways they observed the holiday traditions.

Maggie acknowledged that how purposeful she was in raising her son with such an awareness of both his cultural identities was partly a result of her interactions with multicultural people in Canada and partly due to her academic interests. This was not only evident through her responses but also through the selection of pictures she sent to the researcher after the interview. Alongside the previously discussed photographs, she also sent pictures of her son in her home surrounded by carefully selected books, as well as taking part in different activities in Korea while watching significant Canadian political and sporting events on a television or computer. A final picture depicted her son participating in a typically Korean activity with his kindergarten classmates. In a caption for the picture she draws attention to how her son's pose and expression illustrate to her that he is retaining something of himself in that setting.

Maggie described the "mental load" it required in order to not only maintain her culture and language but also to pass it onto her child. She described the effort required as exhausting and noted how important it was to have others to help. But she also saw the effort as necessary in order for her to retain what was important to herself and help her son understand one aspect of his identity.

> Just because it's hard doesn't mean that you stop doing it. It's who you are . . . If I didn't put effort into it then I would completely lose myself. So I would rather be exhausted sometimes by the burden of it than lose myself and the potential of my child to feel comfortable and confident about part of himself. (Maggie)

From her response Maggie's values in terms of acculturation into Korean society as a mother immigrant of a biracial, multicultural child were twofold. The effort and intentionality she described was not merely about her level of comfort while living in a host culture, it was also about having her son be able to identify with that aspect of his cultural heritage. This sentiment was also evident in the responses of the other participants.

For Maggie, her ability to return home every summer was an important strategy for refreshing her from some of the "mental load" she described in maintaining her culture and passing it down to her son. Similarly, Jessica, Nicky, and Justine expressed the need to at times "take a break from Korea" for various reasons. For them the visits often served the dual function of grounding both them and their children in their culture. Aside from Sue and Jamie, all of the women indicated that they were able to visit their country of origin somewhat frequently. Whereas Maggie's, Jessica's, Nicky's, and Justine's responses in particular indicated that this was an important aspect of their personal self-care, Andrea disagreed that the ability to visit Canada was a factor in her positive outlook to living in Korea. As mentioned previously, the responses of Dianne and Francis indicated that the value they saw in their visits was in helping with their children's connection to family, culture, and language.

Justine desired to raise her son with an awareness of his cultural heritage but was aware of the challenges to achieving this goal.

> I want my son to have equal knowledge of both his cultures, equal appreciation for both his cultures, but I'm not putting in the effort for that to happen. (Justine)

> I worry that you know, multicultural will not end up being so multicultural in the end. I think he's going to identify very strongly with Korean culture and probably feel very unfamiliar and alienated from Canadian culture and that's sad to me but you know, it's life. (Justine)

The context of this response demonstrated not only the importance of her son's understanding of his cultural heritage, but that for Justine, returning to Canada regularly was an important part of her strategy for educating her son in his Canadian heritage. This was in addition to her own need to be refreshed by her visits. Although she had originally planned to visit every year, her second pregnancy and financial realities had made that difficult.

Whereas Jamie enjoyed the advantage of living in Korea because it afforded her children the opportunity to experience their Korean heritage, it was a struggle when it came to her cultural traditions. She became emotional when she described how her daughters were not able to fully experience their American heritage, illustrating the point by comparing her family's observation of holidays. Although she was aware of the large Easter egg hunts prepared by the expatriate community, that morning she had seen pictures her friends from America had posted on social media with their children and the Easter Bunny. She reflected on how she was unable to share that tradition with her daughters. She elaborated on how she had spent the previous Christmas in America with her daughters and husband, describing how they had participated in traditions and festivities with her family of origin. These were experiences which she lamented she couldn't give them while raising them in Korea.

Similarly, Jessica had been in America with her children the December before the interviews. As a result, she was able to celebrate Christmas as well as her daughter's December birthday there. She also lamented how for her husband and in-laws celebrating birthdays was less about creating a special occasion for an individual than she was accustomed to. She described how when celebrating birthdays in Korea her in-laws and husband would typically celebrate by gathering at a convenient restaurant and buying a generic birthday cake from a Korean bakery. Furthermore, they would combine the celebration of relative's birthdays if the dates were close by. She however desired to place more emphasis on making these special days for the individual. She contrasted this with how she had organized a surprise birthday party with a theme personalized to her daughter's current favorite Disney movie while in America the previous December. Evident not only in her spoken account, but by the pictures she forwarded to the researcher after the interview, she had put a lot of thought and preparation into decorations, food, and even costumes. She had discussed in the interview how in addition to her in-law's preferences for celebrating birthdays, it would be difficult for her to even locate in Korea many of the materials she had used for the party.

These responses need to be balanced by Dianne's previously cited responses, where she had made a conscious choice that recreating these kinds of experiences from her childhood memories was less important to her. Even so, it demonstrates that the way in which holidays, and even birthdays were celebrated was an important consideration for the women in terms of passing on their cultural traditions to their children.

In summary, in relation to acceptance of themselves and their children, the women were aware of Korea's homogeneous self-understanding and wanted their children to take pride in their Korean identity. Many were proactive and vocal not only in wanting their children to take pride in both sides of their cultural heritage but also in adopting practices from Korean culture in addition to the aspects of their culture of origin that they wanted to maintain and pass onto their children. A pastoral counseling approach which seeks to help the women to identify the strengths and resources embedded in their unique immigration story as well as their priorities, seems most suitably applied to the women representing this phenomenon. This was a major reason why a feminist pastoral counseling approach, with its emphasis on empowering the individual while assessing the reality of their context, is outlined in the next chapter.

Chapter 7

FERTILE GROUND FOR DISCUSSION AND PASTORAL CARE APPLICATIONS

AFTER DISCUSSING THE FINDINGS detailed in chapters 4, 5, and 6, this chapter seeks to propose a pastoral care model based on Carrie Doehring's *The Practice of Pastoral Care* by incorporating aspects of Augsburger's *Pastoral Care Across Cultures* and acculturation theory. As with Doehring, it proposes a cross-correlation approach in the sense that it invites and encourages dialogue across disciplines in order to provide as accurate an understanding of the careseeker's context as possible. The metaphor of a tree is used to explore the mother's access to community and support, which played a significant part in her acculturation. This metaphor also purposefully and intentionally draws upon connotations of the family tree but develops it not only in terms of extending understanding of influences on an individual beyond that of the biological family, but to one of potentially mutual rather than unilateral influence. It also frames the caregiving relationship as one of co-gardeners.

7.1 Connecting the Themes

Before continuing onto a more detailed discussion of the women's acculturation, it is important to attempt to graphically demonstrate how the three major themes in the previous chapter fit together. This also reflects the dynamic nature of acculturation. The following diagram is imperfect and incomplete in the way it fails to completely depict how interconnected the themes are in reality. The stories and experiences of the individual participants are highly integrated and rich with different aspects of their experience blending into each other in a way a two-dimensional diagram cannot adequately represent. It would perhaps be best to think of the three themes as wheels which can move independently of each other, enabling different parts of each theme to meet at different points at different moments, at different times, and in particular ways in each of the participant's stories, some with greater and some with less emphasis for different individuals.

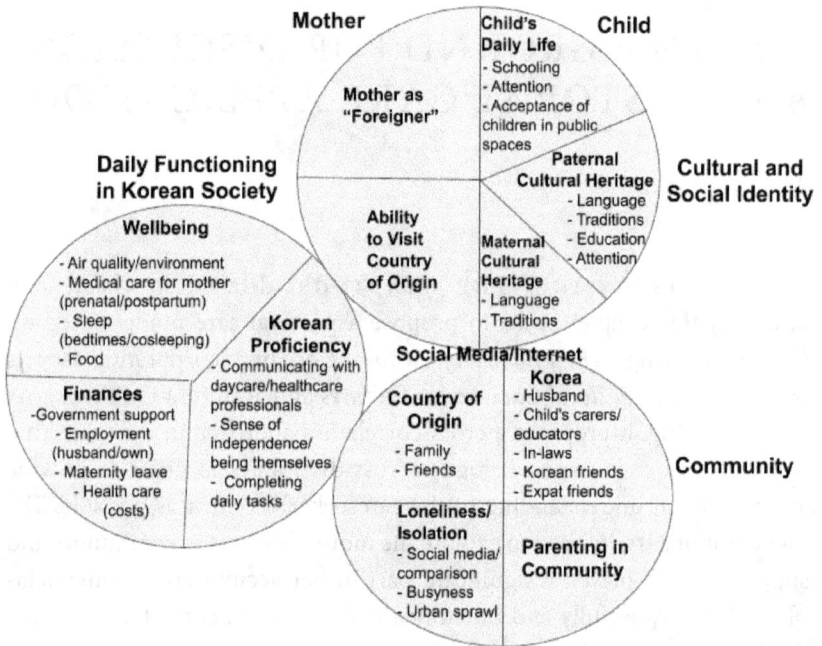

Diagram 4: Themes Wheel

7.2 Acculturation

The themes which emerged in the participant's responses demonstrate not only the dynamic nature of acculturation, but also the acculturation outcomes of behavioral shifts and acculturation stress and strategies of integration as outlined by John Berry. The mothers in the study were all seeking integration which manifested in personalized ways in terms of their choices in behavioral shifts as well as acculturation stress. The women creatively negotiated solutions to acculturation stress in ways which Marc Bornstein's theory can contribute a more nuanced understanding.

The participants described their experience in ways which suggest that they were sensitive to their experience being understood as negative psychological adaption. Berry also sees the tendency to "pathologize" acculturation outcomes as a result of researchers presuming an awareness of a person's individuality and personal preferences which leads them to impose their own ideologies and perspective.[1] The researcher was also sensitive to negative perceptions of multicultural marriages which is what initially prompted the research.

It is important to note that many of the participants described their experiences overall as positive and that many were sensitive to negative assumptions being made about their sociocultural or psychological adaptation. This was perhaps most evident in Andrea's response when she misinterpreted a question as seeking examples of negative experiences only.

> I guess when I think of it as multicultural and you asked me how is day care, I think that oh, maybe it's gonna be harder for him in day care, be more negative because he, suddenly it's another language. (Andrea)

For Maggie the challenges she faced were mediated by her overriding desire for her son to successfully integrate both sides of his cultural heritage and her desire to maintain her own cultural identity.

> I would rather be exhausted sometimes by the burden of it than lose myself and the potential of my child to feel comfortable and confident about part of himself. (Maggie)

In their study on the acculturation stress of marriage immigrant women in Korea, Hyuk Im et al. outline a long list of sources who identify an equally long list of mental health issues common to migrants facing the "mental burden of having to adapt to a new society."[2] Although some of these such as loneliness, feelings of guilt and sadness, anxiety, and even paranoia were specifically mentioned by participants, it did not necessarily define their experience. When engaging expatriate mothers, an over-emphasis or a stereotypical assumption that as immigrants these mental health issues are definitive of their experience, without first adhering to

---

1. Berry, "Living Successfully," 710.
2. Im et al., "Acculturation Stress," 498.

their particular understanding of their experience, could even in fact risk alienating them.

As Bornstein's theory would suggest, the responses of the participants demonstrate that their experiences of immigration and parenting is made complex and nuanced by investment in both host culture and culture of origin with the birth of their child. The experience of motherhood appears to have increased the level at which they were invested in maintaining and participating in both cultures. In some ways, best fit in the sense of what motivates "behavioral change" in Berry's theory was not necessarily the best fit for the greater Korean society but the best fit for each mother and her family.

Just as Sarah Son identified from the responses of the mothers she interviewed,[3] the women in this study were developing their own family culture, at the boundary of two cultures. This new family culture fits Augsburger's understanding of third culture which emerges in the lives of bicultural people.[4] In a similar way, the women in the current study could also be seen actively integrating aspects of Korean culture with their culture of origin in ways which indicated they had been influenced by Western values and notions of multiculturalism, but also personal preferences.

The influence of Western discourses of multiculturalism is most illustrated in instances when the participants expressed belief in the intrinsic value of diverse cultures. Both Charlotte and Francis expressed their appreciation for the school programs aimed at supporting cultural diversity, even if it wasn't specifically related to their own.

> They have multicultural programs where they had different teachers, a Vietnamese teacher come in, a Chinese teacher come in, a Japanese teacher come in, with traditional dress and game and language, and I was really surprised that they had the benefit of getting to try other cultures in their elementary school. (Charlotte)

An understanding of multiculturalism which appreciated diversity was also evident in the importance the women placed on passing on both cultural heritages to their children. In concluding his review of acculturation theory, Bornstein highlights that creating a context where transmission of culture of origin is facilitated in the context of family is potentially "the clearest policy recommendation that has emerged from acculturation

---

3. Son, *National Identity*, 648.
4. Augsburger, *Pastoral Counseling*, 363.

literature."[5] This is a position which the women in the study not only seemed to understand but to varying degrees appeared to be actively striving for.

> I want my son to have equal knowledge of both his cultures, equal appreciation for both his cultures, but I'm not putting in the effort for that to happen. (Justine)

As reflected in Justine's response, despite recognizing the value in asserting effort into maintaining and participating in both cultures equally, other factors of personality and context also influenced the execution in practice.

When considering the *person* as a variable of acculturation, Bornstein includes individual motivation.[6] This is not to say, however, that individuals are not framed in the context of their broader cultural background. This can be seen in contrasting Maggie's and Justine's responses describing their motivation for multiculturalism.

As Canadians, both recognized the value of their children having a grasp of both cultural identities, but they were motivated to varying degrees in the level to which they were actively seeking this as a goal. Despite sharing the goal of their children identifying with both sides of their cultural heritage, personality and preferences were working in a particular way in the case of Anglophone women raising biracial children in Korea.

The women in the current study also described proactive choices of whether or not to adapt to many aspects of life in Korea in relation to everyday issues such as food, language, and cosleeping, which demonstrated a level of openness and awareness to the ways these practices differed from their own. One example was experimentation with cosleeping, which was either embraced as was the case for Francis and Charlotte or rejected as was the case for Andrea. As Berry describes, for many of the women in the study finding a "good fit" for the family in many of these areas was often relatively easy, as in the case of Andrea and her experimentation with and subsequent rejection of what she understood to be the Korean practice of cosleeping.

> That was kind of a different thing that I tried to maybe like, embrace, and adapt to, but my first was the worst sleeper and cosleeping just wasn't that great. (Andrea)

5. Bornstein, "Specificity Principle," 28.
6. Bornstein, "Specificity Principle," 13.

Interestingly, whereas the participants in Son's study reported conflict with their inlaws related to the issue of cosleeping, this was not highlighted in the responses of the mothers in this study. Francis, Charlotte, and Nicky even described happily embracing this practice. Subsequently, although it could initially be understood as an example of the kind of behavioral shift which could be made with relatively little difficulty or conflict,[7] it does appear that other dynamics interact in this process contributing to the level of conflict an adaptation involves.

In other areas of their experiences an element of conflict was necessary in order to find a successful adaptive solution. An integration acculturation strategy, which many of the mothers were applying to varying degrees, depends on a mutually satisfying resolution being found which honors the desires of both parties.[8] This could be seen in the conflict Francis had with her husband and mother-in-law in relation to her children's bedtimes which was ultimately resolved by a bedtime being enforced, but at an hour that accommodated the context of the father returning home later which is common to the Korean context. This example also demonstrates how social and family context work together to affect the integrated acculturated outcome.

Even though adapting to seemly unproblematic low investment behaviors which would be considered reflective of personal tastes and preferences often played out that way for many of the participants, it isn't to say that tension wasn't present in these areas. Out of all the participants, Nicky described the most tensions in her relationship with her in-laws. In particular, she discussed the conflicts which had arisen with her mother-in-law in relation to food and with her father-in-law in relation to discipline. As mentioned previously, her way of reconciling this conflict was to understand it possibly being just as much an indication of generational differences as it was cultural. She reasoned that she had similar disagreements with her mother over certain parenting practices. Similar to the participants in Son's study, Nicky's form of adapted solution was generally to simply go along with the requests of her in-laws only while in their presence provided her son wasn't physically harmed. However, for other participants, food was not a source of conflict at all.

Integrated adaptation was also evident in bigger events such as birthdays and holiday celebrations. Bornstein argues that acculturation is

7. Berry, "Living Successfully," 700.
8. Berry, "Living Successfully," 708.

multidimensional and selective.[9] In the private domain choices are made on the basis of "personal value-related matters of the culture of origin" of which he offers family celebrations as one example.[10] As mentioned previously, the participant's desire for their children to participate in cultural traditions from both sides of their heritage was most often illustrated through the example of holidays. However, the way this played out in the family's life was highly personalized with different elements holding different levels of importance for the women. As Bornstein argues, "Facing the same challenges, different migrants acculturate in different ways."[11]

This was evident in the participant's negotiation of how they celebrated holidays and birthdays with the Korean side of their families and friends with varying levels of success and creative solutions. Jamie, Jessica, and Nicky, for example, were still to varying degrees seeking acceptable resolutions to some of these celebrations, whereas Dianne and Charlotte seemed to be comparatively more settled in their arrangements.

Adaptive solutions to potential sources of conflict were perhaps most evident in the Easter and Halloween events which were especially illustrative of the creative ways the women had found mutually satisfying solutions to their desire to honor their holiday traditions. These held great importance for many of the participants and they were prepared to adjust their expectations in relation to their resources or the needs of others. This was most evident in the celebration of Halloween. Distance from other expatriates and the fact that it wasn't widely practiced, created a barrier to going door to door trick or treating. Using social media to coordinate a gathering in a park where children could dress up and go trick or treating from group to group enabled the women to recreate the experience for themselves and their children in a way which left them feeling like that aspect of their culture had been honored and passed down to their children.

> I feel like it's awesome that he was able to experience the Halloween because now when he watches it, he can relate his experience to what he's watching and he can understand it. (Andrea)

Alternatively, others did not even feel it was necessary to recreate this experience for their children. Modified expectations played a huge part in their overall contentment, which varied between individuals. This was

9. Bornstein, "Specificity Principle," 20.

10. Bornstein, "Specificity Principle," 20.

11. Bornstein, "Specificity Principle," 27.

an important aspect of overall successful psychological adjustment for the mother.

> I don't try to burden myself to make American holidays feel like they would feel in America because I think it takes a whole family to do [that]. (Dianne)

> I think it's just setting yourself up for misery and discontent to even try you know? (Dianne)

The difference in acculturation priorities was also evident in Sue's responses where she doesn't mention the observation of her holiday traditions at all. Many of Sue's responses were distinct in prioritizing more of an assimilation strategy of acculturation, however, she still emphasized how compromise was an important part of what being a multicultural family meant to her. She often avoided conflict by both lowering her expectations and by successfully using non-confrontational ways of addressing issues which were of concern for her to accomplish the desired change. For many of the participants altering expectations extended beyond holidays to making decisions about language and the level to which she wished to be involved in her child's education or even healthcare.

Expectations, particularly those formed through knowledge of Korean culture they had obtained prior to marriage, also affected the interactions with the women's in-laws. As was mentioned in the discussion of the individual themes, tensions in the relationship between the women and their mother-in-laws did not emerge as much as previous research would have indicated. Son's study highlighted that for the women who participated in her study who had become mothers, having children had magnified the conflicts with the mother-in-law over differences in childcare practices in particular.[12] Her participants expressed the tension they felt "between wanting to please their husbands and in-laws, while protecting those things important to their own identity, especially the privacy of their homes" which became "magnified with the birth of the children."[13] She noted how the women in her study often drew on the support of their in-laws due to the distance from their family of origin, which also appeared to exasperate the problem.[14] Her participants described conflicts arising

---

12. Son, *National Identity*, 642.
13. Son, *National Identity*, 642.
14. Son, *National Identity*, 642.

due to the mother perceiving the practices of the in-laws as either unsafe or outdated.[15]

The responses of the current study demonstrate how problematic it could be to carry any assumptions of the nature of the conflict into an understanding of the women's relationship with their in-laws. Sue even expressed her disappointment with the fact that her in-laws were not more involved in her children's lives. This was expressed in ways which not only suggests more of an assimilation strategy but also that her experience was being influenced by her prior understanding of Korean culture. In addition, Jamie described how her in-law's involvement was minimal due to their age. Many of the other participants did not even mention their relationship with their in-laws as a significant part of their motherhood experience. This indicates that for the majority of the participants it was not considered a central aspect of their parenting experience. It could also again be an indication of individual personality and personal preferences but also age and life stage which Bornstein recognizes as variables influencing acculturation.[16]

In contrast to Son's findings, despite being given the opportunity to describe both the advantages and disadvantages of their motherhood experience in Korea, when in-laws were mentioned, it was normally in response to the question of advantages. In particular, Andrea, Francis, and Dianne who appeared to draw most heavily on the support of their in-laws described the relationship and support quite positively. Both Dianne and Francis described how their openness to learning from their in-laws and the Korean culture more generally had facilitated their positive experience. Son saw this process of understanding the rationale behind the practices as a form of acculturation[17]. As indicated in Francis's responses, some of these solutions were the result of initial conflict, which suggests that the length of time of both living in Korea and being a family had contributed to finding satisfactory solutions. Furthermore, in Francis's case, tension was now manifesting in this relationship with her mother-in-law in unexpected ways.

As previously mentioned, Francis, who lived with her widowed mother-in-law, described the history of their relationship as being somewhat challenged by the birth of her children, but also described the care and support she had received from her at that time. Acculturation stress in her

15. Son, *National Identity*, 642.

16. Bornstein, "Specificity Principle," 13.

17. Son, *National Identity*, 642.

case was related to her mother-in-law and no longer in relation to which parenting practices were preferred. It manifested in a shift in values and the resulting conflict she felt between the physical discomfort her and her sons were experiencing due to the pollution levels in Korea and a sense of obligation and responsibility to her mother-in-law who she acknowledged had supported her so much.

> But it's like that Korean mother thing you know? When she gives too much and then you feel guilty your whole life. It's like you have to give it back I think. All Koreans feel that. Don't they? (Francis)

Despite prioritizing her son's cultural and linguistic fluency from both sides of their heritage, there had been a shift in her values, which had been directly influenced by her specific relational experience within the context of her family. Combined, all of these examples demonstrate the need to be sensitive to any preconceived assumptions about the women's preferences and how Western values are expressed in her personal context.

7.2.1 Significance of Being an Anglophone Mother

Bornstein claims that the cultural heritage of immigrants coming from outside what is dominant in the host culture can sometimes be seen as a disadvantage.[18] However, citing others, he also argues that "each culture provides its members with funds of knowledge, tools, norms, and ways of thinking that can contribute to immigrants' engagement in and learning from program activities."[19] Many of the women in this study had benefited from the understandings of multiculturalism from their countries of origin, in ways which reflected Western values but also their relative economic and social status. Their understanding of multiculturalism was an asset in the sense that the participants showed not only a desire to seek understanding but an appreciation of the complexities of the unique cultural dynamics at work in Korean society. Furthermore, the agency expressed in their acculturation often, although not always, emerged in terms of goals which reflected Western values of achieving a multicultural identity for their children which was equally recognized and accepted as integrated in Korean society. This was also expressed in terms of the emphasis the participants

18. Bornstein, "Specificity Principle," 28.
19. Morland; Villarruel et al.; cited in Bornstein, "Specificity Principle," 28.

placed on their children's acceptance into Korean society and competency in their Korean heritage, of which their bilingualism was one aspect.

As previously mentioned, Son correctly highlights that in the context of Korea, Anglophone women benefit from a racial hierarchy, English as a source of social capital, and the perception of socioeconomic equality which distinguishes them from the majority of the female immigrant spouses in Korea.[20] The current study supports this claim with a clear majority of the women being employed in either universities or other English education positions while the participants who were not were proactively choosing domestic labor rather than employment outside the home. Disparities in economic status have been a widely accepted factor influencing marriage migration between developing and developed countries,[21] which makes even this perception of economic equality an important factor influencing the Anglophone mother's experiences as a marriage immigrant.

The women in the current study were aware of how their status factored into their experience, not only in relation to their own employment but their husbands also. Dianne, who was employed as an English professor, acknowledged how both her employment conditions and that of her husband had contributed to her overall satisfaction with life in Korea.

> I do wanna acknowledge my privilege because I think I have a comfortable life here. And that has to do with my husband being a teacher with great hours, he has tenure (Dianne).

This awareness is also suggested in one of the reasons Charlotte gave for not accessing a number of the services offered by the multicultural center in her area. She perceived them as a limited resource which other families in her area could benefit from more than hers. Hence, awareness of their economic and social status was factoring into how the Anglophone expatriate mothers in this study understood their experience. This does not necessarily mean that the women didn't have financial concerns, but rather that they were in a position to explore a number of opportunities as a result of their status, as is demonstrated in Jamie's case in starting her own business.

Other evidence from both previous studies and the responses of the participants also support Son's claim of the relatively high social status allocated to Anglophone women. Despite feminist studies suggesting

---

20. Son, *National Identity*, 633–34.
21. Park et al., "Social Constructions," 110.

the unexpected ways Southeast Asian marriage migrants were exercising agency in Korea, surveys conducted by the Korean Ministry of Health and Welfare found that large numbers of marriage immigrants from Asia did in fact encounter high levels of violence and various forms of abuse.[22] Hyun-sil Kim makes the possible connection between the findings and the prevalence of commercialized marriage introduction services, suggesting that beginning a marriage this way potentially contributes to an abusive marriage dynamic.[23] "The prevalence of abuse is likely to be related to the commercialized marriage process, which may create the idea that the female has been 'purchased' by the family, and is therefore a property rather than a human being."[24]

The dynamics of economic status and social capital can be seen contributing to differences in acculturation between the two demographics of marriage immigrants in Korea both within the family and in the wider society in less dramatic ways as well. The same study on the health of marriage migrants in Korea found that for Southeast Asian brides, cultural differences were often "exasperated by the fact that family members often have little interest in the female migrant's home country and native culture."[25] This contrasts with the women in the current study, as none described or lamented their husband's or in-law's lack of interest in their culture. The descriptions that the participants gave of integrating and adjusting holiday traditions, in particular, suggests that this wasn't the case for Anglophone women, even if satisfactory solutions weren't perfectly executed as of yet. Even in terms of Jamie's experience, the challenge was not her in-law's lack of willingness to participate in her cultural traditions, but rather difficulties in understanding the nature of them. The findings of the current study suggest that the Anglophone mother's culture, traditions, and preferences were respected within the context of the family allowing her to build a cultural context in the home which contributed to her overall positive psychological adjustment. This respect for the Anglophone mother's priorities as well as slightly differing motivations for the bicultural identity of their child is illustrated in Maggie's response.

> I think I, because I am very strong in caring about my culture
> and my language and making it at the forefront, my husband goes

22. Kim, "Social Integration," 563.
23. Kim, "Social Integration," 564.
24. Kim, "Social Integration," 564.
25. Kim, "Social Integration," 565.

along with that because I'm a stronger personality than he is in that. But at the same time, he wants to be able to speak his own language to his child. And he wants his child to succeed academically. (Maggie)

Potential employment opportunities also further extend the differences between Anglophone women and Southeast Asian women. Kim suggests that even professionally trained marriage migrants from Southeast Asia often find a decrease in their socioeconomic status when arriving in Korea due to limitations in their employment opportunities.[26] More recent studies found Southeast Asian female marriage migrants had high levels of unemployment.[27] Furthermore, other studies found that employment of Southeast Asian migrants was heavily dependent on their Korean proficiency with ethnically Korean Chinese women having the highest levels of employment as a result of their higher proficiency.[28] Widely described as the most autonomous of all the Southeast Asian brides,[29] Freeman sees the Korean Chinese marriage migrants as utilizing their agency and improved economic status to achieve goals which are more orientated to values of filial piety.[30] She interprets filial piety towards their family of origin as motivating the predominance of the practice of sending large amounts of money to their families in China, often a source of conflict in their marital home.[31] Marriages and acculturation goals for the Anglophone women in the study reflected Western values even if they expressed these in diverse ways. This suggests that despite the emphasis on individual differences and context indicated in Bornstein's theories, comparisons can be made supporting the claim that Anglophone women have a different migration experience from marriage migrant women from Southeast Asia.

The way the women in this study understood their responsibility toward their children was often expressed in terms of Western understandings of family and society which were outlined in chapter 2. "The function of the family of origin is to launch the developing individual . . . of the

---

26. Kim, "Social Integration," 565.

27. Kim et al., "Fair Treatment," 5.

28. Lee et al., "International Marriages," 178.

29. Lee et al., "International Marriages"; Freeman, *Making and Faking Kinship*.

30. Freeman, *Making and Faking Kinship*, 66.

31. Freeman, *Making and Faking Kinship*, 62, 66.

community to provide a secure, open social context for individual achievements and self-realization."[32]

Although not specifically directing his statement towards immigrants from multicultural families with one parent from the destination culture, Bornstein describes a typical tendency for immigrant parents to:

> desire their children to be successful in the new culture, and their children's abilities to speak the new culture's language, to form positive relationships with new culture peers and others, and to understand nuances in how members of the new culture think and behave are all indications of successful attainment of this goal.[33]

As mothers of biracial children, the participants' emphasis on these factors was not necessarily success in and of itself but held additional meaning. It was important to them that their children would be able to engage with what they saw as an important part of their cultural identity and heritage. In this sense, successful integration of the child not only represented the mother's own successful sociocultural and psychological adaption as it may potentially be understood from a stance of more communal values, but it was also a reflection of standards of Western mental health which prioritizes "an internal sense of personal identity."[34]

The women in the current study expressed their understanding of the obstacles they faced in terms of being fully accepted into Korean society and the impossibility of being recognized as truly "Korean." It is important to note their context as a time in Korean history where previous cultural narratives of homogeneity are being challenged and society is negotiating the societal implications of the form of multiculturalism which is emerging. Subsequently, the issue of their acceptance into Korean society cannot be completely understood outside of the context of this moment of Korean history. Facing this challenge, the women expressed concerns for the implications this had for their child's Korean identity. In many ways this influenced Sue's application of an assimilation strategy, where she didn't discuss passing on her Australian cultural traditions to her children in her responses. Through her descriptions of experiences with her daughter in particular, her assimilation strategies could be understood in terms of her desire not to contribute further to her daughter being perceived differently and from a desire for her daughter to be seen as fully integrated. Her

32. Augsburger, *Pastoral Counseling*, 364.
33. Bornstein, "Specificity Principle," 22.
34. Augsburger, *Pastoral Counseling*, 319.

responses overall also reflected that despite showing the most assimilation of the all the participants, Sue understood her role as a mother in the family of origin as providing a setting for her daughter to flourish holistically.

Similar concerns for the child's successful integration into Korean society are also illustrated in Charlotte's repeated reframe of her objective to raise good Korean citizens.

> I often don't think about raising my children as multiracial. I'm trying to raise them as good Koreans. Canadians second. (Charlotte)

Her active involvement in coordinating the holiday gatherings for the expatriate community suggests her dual priorities of raising children who were well integrated into Korean society but who were also culturally aware of both sides of their heritage. Again, her desire for a Korean identity for her children that also acknowledged their Canadian culture, reflects understandings of Western multiculturalism. Similarly, the participant's connection with the expatriate community, while still related to their personal satisfaction with life in Korea, also became a valuable source of passing on the traditions of their culture of origin for many of the participants.

7.2.2 Evidence of the Specificity Principle of Acculturation

Despite being influenced in their integration strategies by Western values in many ways, the women could be seen negotiating cultural values in ways which suggest Bornstein's theory of acculturation. In as much as the women described differences with in-laws and Korean society in general, the participants also described how their adoption of Korean practices, or even the different context they were parenting in, had also to some extent differentiated and at times put them at odds with their own mothers. Despite differences with their mothers, what emerged as the immigrant bride becomes a mother is not a disconnection to their culture of origin per se. In the process of actively choosing what aspects of their culture to maintain and pass on or pass over, and persisting to do so despite obstacles, they begin to take fresh ownership of their own cultural heritage and that of their host culture.

As they were welcomed into a Korean family, the participants in the study became more intimately involved in cultural traditions. The descriptions they gave suggest that their status as a mother, being included in a family of the destination society, could be understood as fitting in with

Bornstein's specificity principle of setting. As demonstrated by Jamie's experience, Korean traditions took on additional meaning once children were born into the family. The women became invested in Korean society and language in a deeper way as they became mothers in Korea and sought to ensure their children learnt that aspect of their cultural heritage as well.

Along with these factors which can be understood as setting conditions, and the previously mentioned personal factors such as economic status and individual preferences, the specificity principle of time was also influencing aspects of the participant's experience. Understood through the specificity principle of time, the women benefited from migrating at a period of history where they were able to easily maintain access to their culture of origin both via travel and the internet, particularly social media. The mothers participating in the study described their return visits to their country of origin as serving various purposes of maintaining a connection between them and their children to their culture and family of origin. Financial, employment, and for Jessica, even personal concerns for restrictions placed on eligibility for receiving government support, were also important factors which were working together to influence both the duration and the frequency of these trips. In these ways the more nuanced understanding of acculturation offered by the specificity principles Bornstein's theory proposes create a deeper understanding of how various factors can be working together, contributing to the degree to which a mother seeks to maintain and participate in her culture of origin and destination culture. Subsequently, an awareness of how this impacts the mother's sociocultural and psychological acculturation should necessarily be incorporated into an individual's plan for pastoral care.

7.3 Co-Gardener of the Relational Tree: A Model for the Expatriate Mother's Care

The participants expressed different needs and expectations for how the different cultural traditions and heritage would be played out and represented in the daily lives of their family. The values and priorities they held were a reflection of their acculturation. In other words, their values and expectations had been influenced by their level of exposure and acceptance of different aspects of Korean culture. Therefore, the pastoral care approach proposed here begins with listening to the individual's narratives about family and community. It is distinguished from Doehring's approach in how it proposes a culturally sensitive interpathic care on the part of the caregiver.

Augsburger concludes his work on intercultural pastoral care by alluding to a number of metaphors which can be used to understand the pastoral care relationship.[35] Although all metaphors have their limitations, the model proposed here introduces an understanding of the caregiver as co-gardener. In this sense the caregiver, as gardener, works alongside the careseeker, also respecting the individual skills that they bring to the relationship, in order to work together to find adaptive solutions which will help the careseeker flourish within their new setting. Depending on the interpathic discovery within the caregiving relationship, they may utilize a number of different tools (clinical and pastoral skills as well as other resources) to achieve this. This process is visually illustrated in diagram 6 which follows the discussion.

7.3.1 The Relational Tree of the Expatriate Mother

From the participants' responses a number of significant relationships emerged which can be understood as branches of a metaphorical relational tree (see diagram 5). The relational tree is central to the pastoral care model proposed in diagram 6. The branches of the relational tree cross geographical borders or physical proximity which as previously discussed, the internet and travel played a factor in facilitating. Even so, the relational tree is intentionally laid out with the women's networks which have more of a connection to her country of origin represented on the left of the diagram, while those in her support network with more of a connection to Korea such as child carers and educators are on the right. The expatriate community is purposefully near the center of the tree to reflect potentially closer physical and cultural proximity due to the fact that the other expatriates the mother interacts with will also be blending and integrating two or more cultures in various ways. Although intentionally laid out this way, it would be a complete misinterpretation of the model to understand this as a rigid Eastern/Western cultural divide. All the branches of the relational tree are after all just that—branches of the one tree. As such they are irrevocably intertwined in the mother's experience, growing and changing together. From an acculturation understanding, the integration is not a matter of the relative emphasis she is placing on maintaining her culture of origin in

35. Augsburger, *Pastoral Counseling.*

contrast to participating in the new culture. It seeks rather to understand how the different aspects of her community are working together to contribute to her experience.

The left side of the relational tree illustrates the way the mother's relational connections to her country of origin are influencing her motherhood experience as an expatriate. This extends beyond her family of origin (potentially even including extended relatives), to friends. Individual differences such as the length of time she has resided in Korea and also the diversity of the community in which a woman grew up in will influence her sense of a need for connection to friends back home. Furthermore, a woman's connection to an expatriate community also falls into this side of the relational tree. As demonstrated in the participants' responses, a woman will have different priorities for connecting with these different groups which a pastoral carer needs to assess by listening to her stories. Furthermore, this is not static. As demonstrated by Francis, who found she needed the support of the expatriate community less over time as her children grew older, what an expatriate mother seeks in her community can also change over time. Another important consideration is how the relationships on this side of the relational tree are often facilitated by the internet and social media.

The fact that many of the women in the study sought out community via social media has implications for a pastoral care assessment. Due to physical distance, it was often the major (although not necessarily exclusive) way through which connection to the left side of the relational tree was maintained. The need to factor in this aspect of community is especially important, given that the participants themselves were actually aware of both its positive and negative potential. Even more specifically, in the case of Jamie, it occasionally became a source of tension in her relationship with her husband. In other cases, such as Charlotte, it can also be a source of discontent as they see friends in their country of origin living the kind of life that they wish they could have with their family. In an increasingly social media influenced world where, as Bornstein correctly claims, people are increasingly living as expatriates away from their country of origin for various reasons and lengths of time,[36] this platform should not be underestimated in an assessment of an expatriate careseeker's community.

The right side of the relational tree accounts for the social connections which the mother has established geographically in her destination culture,

36. Bornstein, "Specificity Principle," 3.

Korea. This includes in-laws as well as carers and educators, which in the current study took the form of day care, kindergarten, and elementary school teachers. The participants' responses again demonstrated how the careseeker may have different expectations of how they wish to engage with and make use of these branches of the relational tree which may or may not be satisfied. One example from the current study would be Andrea's gratitude for her parent-in-law's support in contrast to Sue's relative disappointment as her original expectations of support didn't match the reality of her parents-in-law's involvement. This can also extend to support from other members of the husband's family.

The fact that language plays a part in navigating these interactions was most clearly demonstrated through the participant's negotiation of their communication with their child's school, but it is not limited to that. This is not to say that language is the only mediating factor, but it was significant in enough of the cases to warrant including it as an important factor of engagement. Particularly when considering carers and educators, it is significant that the women recognized the important role their child's teachers and education more generally were playing in helping their child become connected to their Korean heritage and cultural traditions. Furthermore, although predominantly referring to teachers, the category of carers can also extend to health-care professionals such as pediatricians, obstetricians or gynecologists. Importantly, Bornstein cites a number of studies which demonstrate, particularly in the case of women, that the adaption of the attitudes and values of the culture of destination are related to the level of understanding they have gained from their interactions with the education, welfare, and health-care systems in their host country.[37] As mentioned previously, what is of interest is not assessing the extent to which a woman has crossed over a metaphorical line in order to be considered assimilated into her husband's culture. What is more important from the perspective of a pastoral care assessment is her sociocultural adjustment in terms of her level of comfort in accessing and understanding these systems.

The final two categories on the right side of the relational tree are Korean friends and Korean society more generally. Although not dominant, the responses of the participants reflected on the importance of relationships with Koreans outside their families with varying levels of emphasis for each of the participants. Francis relied on her Korean friends to keep up with information from her son's school. Maggie and Justine noted how

37. Bornstein, "Specificity Principle," 22.

they could potentially benefit from more Korean friends, while also acknowledging the language barriers which often hindered this. In addition, Dianne noted the value of developing friendships with Koreans due to the transient nature of the expatriate community. Furthermore, it is important to evaluate the mother's feelings towards how her children are received more generally in Korean society which was demonstrated in the numerous playground illustrations described by many of the participants. It factors into psychological adjustment considerations in terms of the extent to which the mother recognizes and is comfortable with parenting in a more communal context.

In the relational tree model proposed here, the husband is given a central position in the middle of the left and right spheres directly above the trunk. This is due to the fact that the mother's marriage to her spouse is central to what makes her parenting experience crosscultural. This is not primarily a marriage counseling model and so the presence of the spouse in this pastoral care assessment is more directed at determining the level of support or tension he provides. When considering the husband's part in the relational tree, factors such as employment and domestic roles may or may not need to be taken into consideration both in terms of relational expectations but also in terms of the implications it has on household finances. *Finances* after all, was a subtheme of *Daily Functioning in Korean Society*. Essentially, the husband is given his own branch at the center of the relational tree due to the complexities of their relationship as spouses. Furthermore, whereas language played a factor in other aspects of the "Korean" side of the relational tree, it was not being used in the same way with the husband as it was with these other branches. Language, as it was discussed in relation to the women's spouse, was more related to the level of support she needed from him in communicating with their child's other caregivers. It was also discussed in terms of shared family linguistic goals in relation to the child's bilingual development.

In concluding remarks about the relational tree, it is important to realize that it grows and evolves. This has two implications. Firstly, the branches listed here are not exhaustive. Other important connections and relationships may emerge while listening to the woman's story. Secondly, just as the woman's values and priorities may change, the importance of each branch may grow or diminish for her in a particular season of her life. This metaphor is rich with imagery to help a woman understand seasons in relationships where certain branches may need to be pruned, may die back and lose their leaves for a period or may flourish at other times. As a co-gardener, the caregiver's first step is to interpathically assess the dynamics of the woman's relational tree.

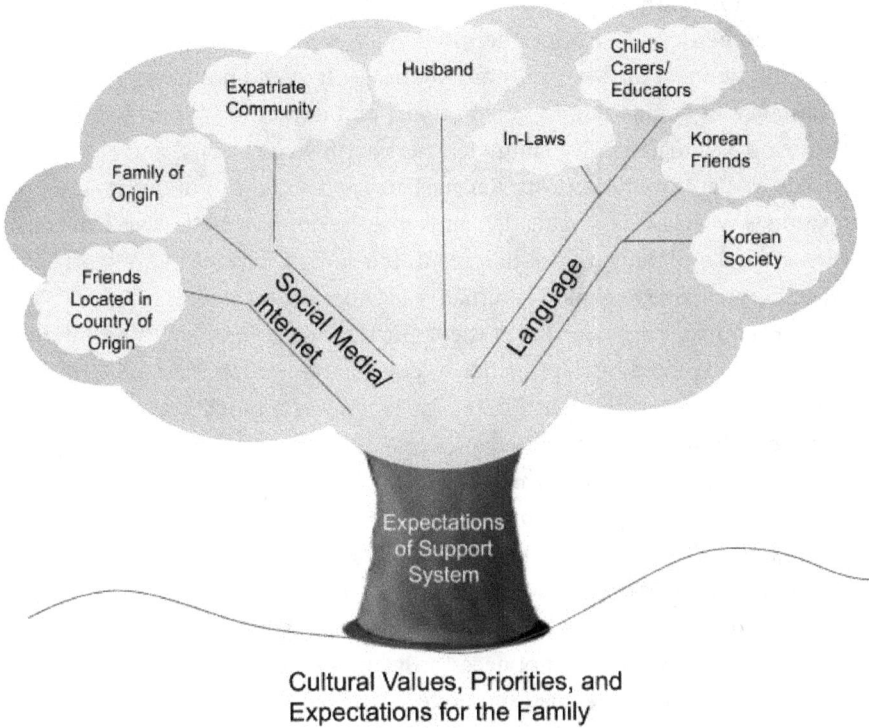

Cultural Values, Priorities, and
Expectations for the Family

Diagram 5: The Relational Tree of the Expatriate Mother

7.3.2 Interpathic Listening and Psychological Assessment

Having introduced the relational tree, the following section will outline the steps of the proposed co-gardener pastoral care model which is illustrated in diagram 6. The pastoral care model proposed here begins with inter-pathic listening. The clearest argument for the need for interpathic pastoral care in the case of Anglophone immigrant mothers emerges in descriptions of Sue's experience, as she describes the disconnection with the professional care she received in Australia after being diagnosed with PPD following the birth of her first child.

> Whatever cultural sensitive, sensitivity training they may have
> or may not have, they cannot apply it to when they experience

someone who is Australian by all senses but is in an intercultural marriage that, that it doesn't reflect their standard attitude of what marriage is. (Sue)

An interpathic carer would have bracketed preferences for Sue to demand domestic support from her husband as well as any assumptions that this was her goal for her family and marriage. It would not have seen Sue's resistance to demanding more emotional and domestic support from her husband as a maladaptive failure to assert her own emotional and physical needs in a confrontation with her husband and sought to understand the reason why she was assessing demands that she do so as ineffective. Having recognized and valued Sue's judgment, the caregiver would have worked together with Sue to explore alternative avenues for emotional support.

Had a care provider taken the approach of a co-gardener and interpathically explored Sue's priorities in developing her family culture, they would have discovered that Korean language was a practice that she had strategically and intentionally adapted for her family's situation after weighing up alternative options. This potentially would have led them to explore the option of a support group with Korean immigrant mothers in her area. The fact that this occurred in Australia, and not in Korea, suggests that acculturation, particularly within the family context, is in many ways the creation of a third culture that the individual is carrying within them and their community which is not necessarily limited to geographical location.

The location of the care exasperated the situation in how it contributed to Sue's care provider's assumptions about her values and priorities. For this reason, it highlights a key characteristic of an interpathic co-gardener care provider—an awareness of their presumptions and preferences for the outcomes for the careseeker and their community. Secondly, it requires them to actively put those preferences aside. It then requires them to uphold and respect the validity of the careseeker's position through an active awareness and reflection on moments when the careseeker is describing and displaying unexpected preferences or values.

Approaching an expatriate mother's experience as an interpathic co-gardener can potentially lead to creative understandings of the different forms her community can take and the way she draws on them. In examining the acculturation stress among marriage migrants in Busan, one study had participants complete a questionnaire addressing "sociodemographic factors, acculturation stress, coping resources, and mental health."[38]

38. Im et al., "Acculturation Stress," 499.

It considered social support and satisfaction as coping resources and recommended the implementation of programs such as "self-help groups" which would facilitate social support.[39] In providing pastoral care, it appears to be necessary to look beyond the generalized need for a supportive community to exploring the various forms the communities take, the careseeker's expectations of these communities, and whether these expectations are either met or left unfulfilled. As demonstrated in the responses of the participants, the answer to these questions are both personalized and linked to the mother's experience of acculturation.

Son also found that for the Anglophone women in her study, social participation played a part in their overall satisfaction with daily life.[40] Where language barriers and lack of commonality created barriers to relationships with Koreans, the women tended to draw on relationships with other expatriates.[41] For the women in this study, social media platforms were an important part of creating a community in which social participation could occur, particularly with other expatriates. Due to the busyness of motherhood and in many cases employment, many of the women in the current study were creating a sense of community online. In addition, the participants in the current study relied heavily on social media as a way to maintain communication and connection to their culture of origin. Specifically, they utilized this online community for support and encouragement, information, and at times tangible resource exchange, but also in order to coordinate celebrations which were significant to them.

For many of these reasons, both Jamie and Justine described social media as a "lifeline." For Justine it became an important outlet for her acculturation stress and the sole way she was able to overcome her PPD.

> There have been a couple of times when I have. When I've really been kind of beyond and I've just felt like it's just been such a wonderful release and the women are so supportive. (Justine)

Justine acknowledged that she may also have been susceptible to the condition had she given birth in Canada, but identified the context of parenting in Korea as exasperating the experience.

> I believe it was exasperated by being in Korea, where I didn't really have a support system. (Justine)

39. Im et al., "Acculturation Stress," 497–98.
40. Son, *National Identity*, 645.
41. Son, *National Identity*, 645.

For her, the online community within Korea and staying connected to her family back home was her primary way of coping with her PPD.

The second step in the pastoral care model outlined in diagram 6 is an assessment of the careseeker's relational tree. As described in chapter 2, Doehring's model of pastoral care proposes two questions in making an assessment of family, community, and culture: "In what ways do these relational systems help the careseeker mourn losses, survive violence, and cope with stress? Do any of them intensify her suffering?"[42] In making an assessment of the expatriate mother which is sensitive to her acculturation process three more questions are proposed. Firstly, what access to support networks and community does she have? Secondly, what are her priorities and expectations for these communities and how does she wish to draw on them? Finally, how are the relationships contributing either positively or negatively to the woman's adjustment and acculturation stress? This final question begins to transition into the third step of the co-gardener model, a psychological assessment. The relational tree metaphor proposed is based on the premise that the woman's relationships have contributed to both her sociocultural and psychological acculturation adaptation. Subsequently, in order to understand the nature of any acculturation stress, it is first necessary to understand the roles these relationships have in her experience.

The foundation of the tree metaphor starts by examining the way a woman's priorities and values have been influenced by acculturation. This can be understood as the soil in which the metaphorical relational tree is planted. As an expatriate married into a family of the destination country, the mother is both connected to the host culture and will have varying levels of access to different forms of community and support. Even if the women in the study had not consciously articulated them prior to the interview, they expressed particular goals and expectations for their family. These were in terms of hopes for their children to feel confident in their cultural heritage and languages, how their families observed holidays, and even the foods that were eaten. The women were engaging with their context, evaluating choices they were presented with, and made decisions based on these evaluations, whether this was a decision based on the comparative benefits or limitations to which food to serve or which holidays to observe. They were considering and negotiating not only their own needs and desires but that of their Korean family and context.

42. Doehring, *Pastoral Care*, 97.

Interpathic dialogue is important to understanding the priorities an Anglophone expatriate mother has for maintaining her culture of origin and participating in Korean culture, and how this may or may not be contributing to her acculturation stress. This discussion can begin as casually as asking her about what she enjoys about living in Korea and what she misses about her culture of origin. More formally, asking what she sees as the advantages and disadvantages of raising her children in the host culture or working with her (and potentially her husband if he is willing and it seems beneficial) to identify and reevaluate a list of family values, could also be an instigator for exploring the soil of the relational tree. The priorities the mother places on the different aspects of the cultures and social engagement, contributes to her satisfaction or disappointment and is an important starting place to understanding her communities.

In this sense, the idea of social identity is also being used slightly differently than the way in which Doehring proposes. She sees social identity as an aspect of assessing the careseeker's families, communities, and cultures, an important part which she sees as "determining whether aspects of her identity are positively regarded and give her access to material, psychological, and social resources."[43] It is not that Doehring doesn't see cultural context as important to understanding the formative role it plays in the careseeker's social identity, but her emphasis is placed on the ways this has contributed to social privilege or disadvantage.[44] As mentioned previously, this is a factor in the acculturation process which has been argued often differentiates the Anglophone marriage immigrant to the experiences of Asian marriage immigrants in Korea, specifically in relation to how the immigrant's culture is valued in their marital home. This will provide an element of insight into the mother's acculturation stress, but it is only one aspect. In making an assessment of an expatriate mother, a careseeker in an intercultural marriage, it is also important to listen to her story to understand how she articulates her priorities for maintaining and participating in the two cultures, as well as how she has been impacted, influenced, and supported by both.

Once the foundation of the relational tree has been laid by listening to the mother's narratives of what her values and priorities are, the pastoral giver as interpathic co-gardener is in a better position to explore the various communities the woman has access to more deeply and assess how

43. Doehring, *Pastoral Care*, 102.
44. Doehring, *Pastoral Care*, 166.

she could potentially benefit from strengthening various branches of her relational tree or even crafting new ones. If the foundation and soil of the relational tree is the careseeker's expectations and priorities, the trunk is the support system from which different communities that the mother engages with branch off. The Anglophone expatriate mother's values and priorities for her nuclear family are either exasperated or supported to varying degrees by the level of support she can receive from family, friends, and her child's carers and educators. It also influences the part she sees them playing in her motherhood experience.

Through exploring the mother's narrative of her experience through relationships, as well as her understandings of the advantages and disadvantages of her life as an expatriate, a greater understanding for the context of her concerns emerges in ways which relate to the other themes in the participant's responses. In this sense, the model moves towards step 3 of the co-gardener model outlined in diagram 6, a more psychological assessment. For example, what is the nature of her concerns for pollution? Are they related to concerns for the immediate health challenges they present to herself and her family as in the case of Francis? How is the situation exasperated by emotional concerns? As discussed previously, for Francis, who was the most conflicted about the air quality, there were more deeply embedded concerns related to her history with, and subsequent sense of obligation towards her widowed mother-in-law. Again, interpathic understanding is necessary.

Approaching an understanding of Francis's context and concerns for living in Korea with preconceptions shaped by negative expectations of the relationship which would develop between daughters-in-laws and their mother-in-laws having lived together for almost the entirety of the younger woman's marriage, would have missed the nature of Francis's dilemma. An empathetic listener would have easily recognized and related to Francis's descriptions of conflict and tensions from this arrangement, and subsequently acknowledged the difficulties and struggles she faced. Alternatively, an interpathic listener would realize that as a result of these conflicts, Francis's values had shifted and now her discomfort with the quality of air was exasperated by the fact that she felt that she was unable to leave Korea and the poor air quality due to a sense of obligation towards her mother-in-law.

Alternatively, concerns for the air pollution in Korea could be connected to valuing more global concerns for the environment as in the case of Charlotte. The implications for pastoral care solutions for both Charlotte and Francis would differ in terms of the support which could be offered and should also be developed in dialogue with the mother. In this case, acculturation stress could be alleviated by taking proactive action to foster greater environmental awareness both within the family and her broader community. This was indeed the approach Charlotte was taking. This approach also has the potential to uncover other creative solutions.

When examining the different branches in the expatriate careseeker's relational tree, it is important to explore the priorities and expectations they have for communication and support of those in their network. For example, some may be content with minimal contact with their family of origin while others may consider it important to find creative ways to include their family of origin in different aspects of daily life. Maggie demonstrated this in her use of video chat with her mother. Similarly, the mother may have different hopes for the level to which she expects or is expected to be involved in her child's education as well as the way traditional domestic gender roles will be played out in the home with her husband.

In the process of dialogue in the co-gardener relationship, the caregiver can potentially identify the best ways to empower the mother by connecting her to various resources. This is important for the successful implementation of a plan of care which is step 5 in diagram 6. For example, if a mother desires to rely less on her husband in her understanding of the Korean education systems and other forms of government support which are available to her, the caregiver could potentially help her to explore options for sourcing and confirming the information she has through the various support groups offered online, find ways to help her connect with other Korean mothers at her child's school, or even petition for greater access to this information through more official structures. Although many issues may accommodate practical solutions, they will only be temporary until the careseeker is able to reconcile their embedded beliefs about their community alongside their status within their new host society. For this reason, theological reflection suggested in step 4 of the co-gardener pastoral care model provides a useful foundation to step 5, the construction of a plan of care (see diagram 6).

7.3.3 Ruth: Theological Reflections on the Narrative of Ruth

Embedded within the Anglophone mother's acculturation experiences and choices are beliefs she holds about herself and her place in her community. These beliefs reflect the expectations she has of herself and of the systems within which she is embedded. As Doehring's model suggests, these may be heavily rationalized, developed, and deliberative, or they can be so integrated into understanding of the world that they often go unarticulated or explored without any depth.[45] Examining narratives within the Bible which depict other immigrants interacting and engaging with their host community provides an avenue for exploring the careseeker's embedded and deliberative beliefs about themselves and their community.

The expatriate mother is navigating at the border of a different and literal form of cultural divide than is described by Miller-McLemore in her reflection of the narrative. Many of the themes Miller-McLemore highlights in the first chapter of the book of Ruth do indeed have many parallels with the current marriage phenomenon in Korea. She notes how the opening chapters of the book of Ruth find the women widowed and childless in a cultural climate where a woman's status and survival were determined by having both.[46] Although not to this extreme, as demonstrated previously, Korea can be seen allocating the status of marriage migrants to their roles as mother and daughter-in-law.[47] Previous chapters have demonstrated how Korean society is elevating international marriage and multicultural families in an effort to alleviate the strain of a declining birth rate and aging population. As illustrated by Justine, some of the women in the current study were aware of the challenges of the patriarchal system and recognized how the Korean context contributed to gender role dynamics which they wished to challenge.

> I feel like because we live in Korea and because of the very deeply entrenched gender roles here, it's like more, it's easier to just let that happen. (Justine)

Even so, Miller-McLemore's reflection on Ruth has limitations when applied to the Korean context. The women in the study were more focused on how they benefited from the community and their reciprocal sense of responsibility towards their host society. Just as was the case with Ruth,

45. Doehring, *Pastoral Care*, 112.

46. Miller-McLemore, *Also a Mother*, 177.

47. See also Kim, "Gender Construction."

goals of self-actualization for themselves and for their children were best achieved through the system.

Miller-McLemore claims that the emphasis on the mother's house in the book of Ruth signifies the "unifying and solidifying power of the mother."[48] Even though the Korean context is consistent with understanding a patriarchal context, the cultural clash MillerMcLemore describes is not necessarily about the unifying power of the mother. She argues that Orpah's decision to return to her mother's house is a proactive decision to reclaim her maternal past.[49] As seen in the participant's descriptions of their relationships with their mothers and mothers-in-law, the choice is one of negotiation and reconstruction rather than unification. This perhaps articulates the choices facing Anglophone women more accurately as they decide what to hold onto out of both cultures.

The responses of the participants in this study suggest that even if they were to return geographically to their country of origin, the outcome would be more complex than them simply "reclaiming" their "maternal past" as proposed by Miller-McLemore. Unlike the widowed and childless Orpah, the woman tangibly carries her culture of marriage as well as her culture of origin with her wherever she goes. To varying degrees she is emotionally, physically, and spiritually invested in both cultures due to her marriage, motherhood, and her background. This is perhaps best illustrated through the experience of Sue. The Anglophone mother negotiates what it means for her and her children to obtain acceptance and recognition in their destination society. In Korea she navigates language, traditions, distance from support, and the fostering of her child's awareness of their cultural heritage. In addition, she navigates her own expectations, priorities, and preferences as well as the expectations of others. In this sense, Miller-McLemore's observation of being caught "*between* cultures" seems especially rich with literal application. This navigation of both cultures, particularly concerns for the multicultural and linguistic fluency of her child or children, aren't limited to a geographical location and would understandably continue even if she were to "return to her mother's house" as Orpah did. Ruth's experience also has theological implications for the participants in this study.

Like the participants in this study, Ruth actively draws on various relationships in her acculturation experience. From this perspective, the responses of the women in the study echo more of the themes implicated in

48. Miller-McLemore, *Also a Mother*, 178.
49. Miller-McLemore, *Also a Mother*, 178.

Carroll's reflection. Just as he sees Ruth actively utilizing support networks, the women all described the extent to which they were seeking and drawing on various communities. It also reflects how they were understanding the labels that were placed on them and their children as "foreigners" or "English speakers" as they negotiated acceptance of their child's Korean identity but also their own place in Korean society. Ruth overcame these ambiguities and questions about her role and status in the society. Just as Carroll suggests, she took "purposive action" utilizing "networks and forms of human capital" and drew on "institutional mechanisms."[50] Ruth was both benefactor of her host society and worked within systems which ultimately lead to a mutually satisfying outcome. The outcome was satisfying for Ruth in the sense that she achieved her stated objectives in how she wished to fulfill her relational commitment and obligations to her marital home.

In a similar way, working as a co-gardener, a care provider will honor the priorities and preferences the careseeker has for her family. They will seek to interpathically understand those desired outcomes helping her to take purposeful action towards them, and to understand her networks as a form of human capital while working within systems and structures to achieve change and mutually satisfying outcomes. As demonstrated in the previous sections, this process of tending to the immigrant careseeker's relational tree can take a variety of forms which are highly dependent on interpathic dialogue which occurs between two co-gardeners in the caregiving relationship.

Ruth's position in the lineage of Jesus demonstrates that God has a plan and a purpose for women in cross-cultural marriages as well as their families. Consistent with Carroll's reflections on the book of Ruth, a co-gardener care provider has the opportunity to nurture and tend growth which they themselves may not even see to full fruition. Multicultural families should have an accepted place in their community and be given space to become valuable contributors to the society in a reciprocal relationship. They have a right to navigate their cultural space and explore their place in society. A co-gardener's role is to work alongside the women and their communities in order to help them flourish and produce lasting fruit as they nurture their gifts and navigate the transitional season of motherhood and the additional opportunities and resources that their cross-cultural context presents them with.

50. Carroll R., "Once a Stranger," 185.

Caregiver as Co-Gardener

Step 1
Interpathically Listening to Careseeker's Narratives

Step 2
Interpathic Reflection of Careseeker's Relational Tree

1. What access to support networks and community does she have?

2. What are her priorities and expectations for these communities and her role in them?

3. What does she understand to be the advantages and disadvantages of her context?

Careseeker as Co-Gardener

Step 3
Psychological Assessment

1. How have these relationships either contributed to or relieved acculturation stress? In what ways?

2. Are any physical concerns being aggravated by emotional ones? In what ways?

3. What are the narrative's surrounding issues of discomfort? How are they related to her expectations and priorities?

Reconnect with Community

Step 4
Theological Reflection

1. What are the theological implications for the careseeker's understanding of community and themselves?
- Do they have an embedded theology which is influencing their relational expectations?
- To what extent are these embedded or deliberative?
2. Can her understanding of community be reframed in order to improve her adaptation?

Step 5
Plan of Care

1. How can the careseeker be best supported to find adaptive solutions to conflict through external resources or through attending any of the branches of the relational tree?

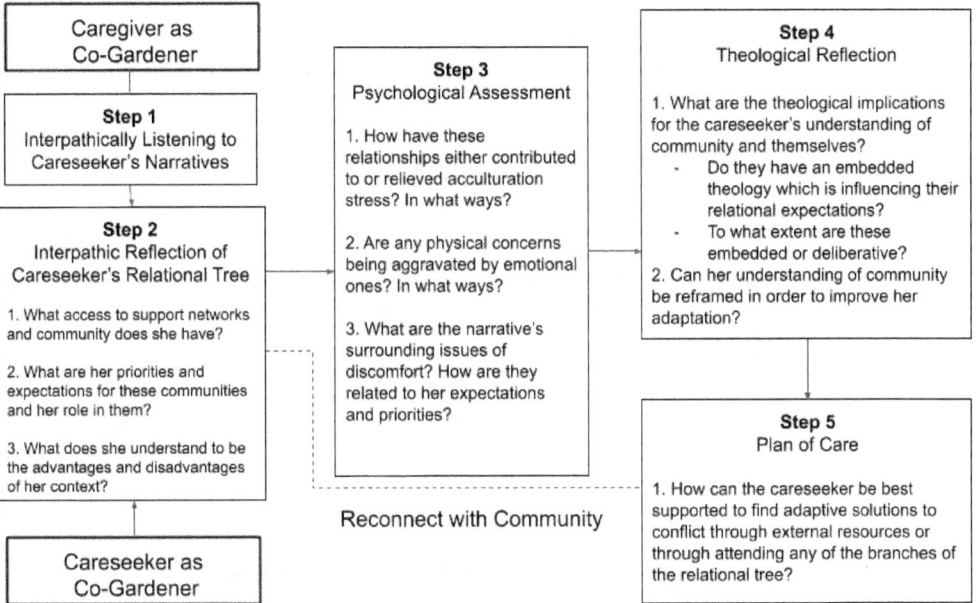

Diagram 6: Co-Gardener of the Relational Tree:
A Model for the Expatriate Mother's Care

Chapter 8

CONCLUSION

THIS STUDY HAS TWO primary objectives. Firstly, it contributes diversity to the current discourse of multiculturalism in Korean society by offering the experiences of Anglophone mothers to the discussion. Whereas much of the dialogue on the emerging multiculturalism in Korea has focused on female immigrant spouses from other parts of Asia, this book takes the unique position of the experiences of Anglophone women from Western nations parenting within an international marriage with a Korean spouse in the context of Korea. Secondly, after presenting a phenomenological study of these mothers, the book explores the application of a feminist pastoral care approach to the findings. As has been demonstrated, the Korean context provides a unique case study as a society negotiating a transition from a homogeneous self-understanding to a developing discourse of multiculturalism.

After describing how international marriages in Korea have caused the society's discourse to shift from one of homogeneity to articulating multiculturalism, chapter 3 outlines the methodology of this particular study. The phenomenological methodology taken here supports the objective of the research which is to study and describe the experience of Anglophone marriage immigrants as they raise their children in Korea. The ten participants described how they navigated social norms, daily routines, and their need for community alongside their priorities of maintaining and passing down cultural traditions and language from both sides of the family's heritage. Consistent with a phenomenological methodology, these themes emerged from the responses of the participants as they discussed their experiences of motherhood as an expatriate in Korea. These themes have been outlined in section 2.

Chapters 4, 5, and 6 detail the themes identified from the participant's motherhood experience. These themes of *Daily Functioning in Korean Society*, *Community*, and *Social and Cultural Identity*, along with various subthemes, emerged as the participants described what they understood as advantages and disadvantages of raising their children in Korea, in addition to articulating what being a "multicultural family" meant to them personally. These themes also emerged from the participant's responses where they reflected on how their expectations of motherhood had changed as they had become a parent in Korea. The three major themes can be seen as interrelated and overlapping in various ways, perhaps most intuitively when considering daily life in Korea and the Korean side of the community diagram (see diagrams 1 and 2).

8.1 Brief Overview of the Findings

The first theme described in chapter 4 is *Daily Functioning in Korean Society*. This theme is best described simply as the aspects of daily life which were a routine part of the participant's motherhood experience in Korea. The description under this theme broadly covered the practical aspects of parenting in Korea in terms of what the participant considered to be benefits and challenges as well as some of the ways she had adopted, adjusted to or declined to adapt to the parenting styles she had been exposed to. This theme was divided into three subthemes of *Wellbeing*, *Korean Proficiency*, and *Finances*. The first subtheme of *Wellbeing* covered the way the participant thought about receiving medical care for herself, particularly in relation to her pregnancy, environmental factors, philosophies on sleep, and the food she ate with her family. The second sub-theme is *Finances*. *Finances* also covered aspects of the participant's experience which were related to health care but with less focus on the care received and more on financial accessibility. Employment and financial assistance from the government were also discussed under this subtheme. The final subtheme is *Korean Proficiency*. Although language was an aspect of the participant's expatriate parenting experience in various ways, this subtheme covered the ways in which Korean proficiency affected routine interactions. It also includes how she saw her proficiency in the Korean language as either an asset or a hindrance both to her sense of self but also in the way it at times empowered or limited her as a parent.

The second theme discussed in Chapter 5 is *Community*. The theme *Community* is loosely separated into those connections located in Korea and those in the participant's country of origin. Although it would be expected that the women would have family and friends located in both their country of origin and Korea, this theme also covered the way that they were utilizing social media and the internet to close the geographical divide with their family of origin and also create community with other expatriates in Korea. Furthermore, it describes how the mothers had come to understand Korean communal social norms, navigated loneliness and isolation, and understood their need for community, support, and connection with family and friends located in their country of origin.

The third theme is *Cultural and Social Identity*. Graphically it is divided into two spheres with the mother on one side and the child represented on the other. The objective of this description is not to provide a detailed analysis of identity formation. Rather, it provides a discussion of the woman's priorities in maintaining and passing on cultural identity as well as their perceptions of their acceptance into Korean society. The participant's reflections are understood as twofold; in terms of how this relates to herself and how they relate to her child or children.

8.2 Implications of the Study

The results of the phenomenological study show that the ten Anglophone marriage immigrants who were raising their biracial children in Korea represent diverse acculturation of values and traditions which Bornstein's specificity principle would suggest. Indeed, the need for this research is based on the assumption that due to differences in culture of origin, language, and status in the destination culture, the Anglophone women will have a different experience of marriage migration and parenting in Korea from the Asian marriage immigrant women who are currently addressed in the majority of the literature. This is also asserted in Sarah Son's paper which is currently the only other work focused on Anglophone marriage immigrants in Korea.

The dynamic of being a non-citizen parenting a child who is a citizen of the destination culture which has been so heavily shaped by a discourse of homogeneity contributes specific conditions which influence acculturation.

This research argues that it is necessary to take these important contextual factors into consideration in order to understand how they have influenced the woman's experience, values, priorities, needs, and expectations. Despite a number of demographic similarities among the participants, they also represented a variety of ways in which they were adopting, adapting to, incorporating or dismissing ideas and norms from both cultures, even if the influence of Western values and understandings of multiculturalism could be identified in their responses. Alongside factors identified by Son, this also appeared to distinguish the women from their Southeast Asian counterparts.

Although with differing emphasis and described in different ways, the women expressed their desire for their children to be recognized and accepted as Korean rather than foreigners even if they themselves were not. Due to the length of time they had resided in Korea, a number of the participants had in many ways come to accept their "foreign" status. Their status as a foreigner was not necessarily a concern for them until they perceived it as a source of discrimination or when it affected their child's acceptance negatively. The participants had similar priorities for their children to identify with, and to take pride in both their maternal and paternal heritage which manifested differently and with different emphasis in each of the families.

Community and support were a significant part of the participant's motherhood experience. Maintaining connection with different communities in various ways helped her to not only pass on culture, language, and traditions, but also played a part in the values and practices she maintained, adopted, or adjusted to. It was also an important way the women navigated feelings of loneliness and isolation. The creative and various ways the women navigated community was evident in the use of social media and the internet. Although not all, many of the women described their social media use in ways which indicated that it is an important part of their expatriate motherhood experience. Not only does a pastoral care provider need to take this into consideration when caring for an expatriate in their congregation, it warrants further investigation.

In addition, the findings suggest a broader application for pastoral care outside of the context of Korea. As Sue's experience of postpartum depression indicates, just because a person is living in their country of origin it cannot necessarily be assumed that their values and priorities have not been influenced by exposure to different cultures. In an increasingly multicultural and globally mobile world, any pastor would surely benefit from an approach which is sensitive to the way a person's background and experience reflect acculturation to varying degrees.

The feminist pastoral care approach described by Carrie Doehring provides the foundation for the model proposed here.[1] This book contributes David Augsburger's notion of interpathy to develop a pastoral model which is sensitive to the different factors influencing a marriage immigration experience which the acculturation theory would suggest. Building on the metaphor of a tree, this book argues for an evaluation of the careseeker's community in light of how her personal narrative and exposure to Korean society has influenced her values and practices. In concluding, it is necessary to address some aspects of the application of Doehring's model and the relational tree metaphor.

Firstly, as previously mentioned, Doehring's model focuses on crisis intervention which could take the form of sudden loss due to a life transition or even violence,[2] but this may not always need to be the focus of pastoral care in this context. While not denying crisis intervention may at times be a factor in the pastoral care of an expatriate mother, it does not necessarily have to be the starting point. The participants' responses did not describe seasons of current transition. In many ways they appeared settled in their experience. As a result, rather than expressing their pastoral care needs in terms of loss or crisis, it seems more appropriate to describe a pastoral approach to their care differently than crisis intervention alone.

In the context of marriage immigrants raising their children in their host culture such as the participants in this study, pastoral care may potentially place a greater emphasis on community building. This may possibly involve providing opportunities for community; places to honor milestones and traditions. It could empower acculturation through helping them identify and articulate various positions, values and resources they inherently bring to their migration experience. Perhaps too often the emphasis on intercultural marriage counseling has been on crisis intervention and the presumption of the need for conflict resolution and identifying points of tension rather than identifying opportunities to empower the couple as individuals and subsequently strengthen the family. While this is clearly within the parameters of clinical counseling, what are the implications for pastoral care? These findings hopefully suggest a new paradigm

1. Doehring, *Pastoral Care*.
2. Doehring, *Pastoral Care*, 7.

to understanding pastoral counseling for these intercultural families. The implications of these findings extend beyond the context of marriage immigrants and potentially to ministry to expatriates in general in an increasingly global world.

What is being emphasized here with the metaphor of a relational tree and co-gardener is not a static model focused on the individual. What is needed is the ability to listen to an individual's story in order to understand and explore how their exposure to different cultures, in this case through marriage and motherhood, has shaped their values, priorities, expectations, and needs. Due to different influences in individual experiences and relationships, this will look different for different individuals. Furthermore, as the individual interacts with those in the branches of her relational tree, her values, expectations, and priorities also evolve. As argued in the previous chapter, God has a plan for planting the women and their multicultural families in their communities. They are planted to belong. The goal of a co-gardener pastoral carer is to support the woman and the community to enable them to flourish.

8.3 Limitations to the Study

As with any study, there are a number of limitations to the current study. In particular, the findings on the mother's use of social media needs to be measured. The method of recruiting participants may have potentially biased the data. The fact that almost 80 percent of the participants specifically mentioned the significance of social media, and Facebook groups in particular, as a notable part of their experience and strategies in raising their children in Korea could be a result of the fact that Facebook groups were the platform through which the participants were recruited. It is most likely that active group members would respond to the request for participants in the research, which may have led to an overrepresentation of the way that social media is integrated into their experience. Aside from two participants, all of the mothers described various ways in which they utilized social media not only in terms of maintaining contact with their friends and family back in their countries of origin, but also for discovering and learning about different events, resources, and importantly for developing a sense of community. Many of the participants were also aware of the potential negative aspects of social media platforms, with some even expressing a desire to quit. It also at times led to comparisons with their communities in their countries of origin that fed feelings of isolation and loneliness, which are signs of acculturation stress.

The timing of the interviews in the data collection may have also influenced other aspects of the participant's responses. Six of the ten interviews were conducted between Monday March 26 and Friday March 30, 2018. Following the lunar calendar, this week happened to be the lead up to the Easter weekend in the year that the interviews were conducted. Three of the other interviews were held in the two weeks prior to this week. Many of the mothers discussed their plans to attend Easter egg hunts which had been organized through various social media groups with other expatriate parents residing in Korea. Some of the women, even while stating that they were not Christian, recognized the cultural significance that this holiday and the various traditions, such as egg dying and going on Easter egg hunts, held for them. Almost all of the women did not limit this discussion to Easter but also talked about the importance of how they celebrated and passed down other various holiday traditions from their culture. It is difficult to say whether the scheduling of interviews around Easter caused them to give greater attention to this than they would have otherwise.

Other events in Korea around the time of the interviews are also worth considering. During the primary week of data collection, air pollution levels in and around Seoul were particularly high throughout Korea with many women lamenting this fact. Graphs 1 and 2 illustrate pollutant levels in Seoul for the month of March 2018 according to the Air Korea website developed by the Korean Ministry of Environment in conjunction with the Korean Environment Corporation.[3] According to the Air Korea website, PM10 and PM2.5 air pollutants peaked in Seoul during March 22 to March 30, which was when 60 percent of the interviews took place. The chart depicts Gangnam-gu, Gangseo-gu, and Jongno-gu which are various areas in Seoul. Gangnam-gu is the southeastern area of Seoul made famous by the Kpop song *Gangnam Style*. Jongno-gu is in central Seoul close to where City Hall and many of the traditional palaces are located. Gangseo-gu is in the western part of Seoul. The chart demonstrates that although there were days with high levels of pollution throughout March 2018, which is typical of that time of year, the levels peaked at their highest during the period when the majority of interviews were held.

3. http://www.airkorea.or.kr

Graphs 1 and 2: PM10 and 2.5 Levels for the Month of March 2018

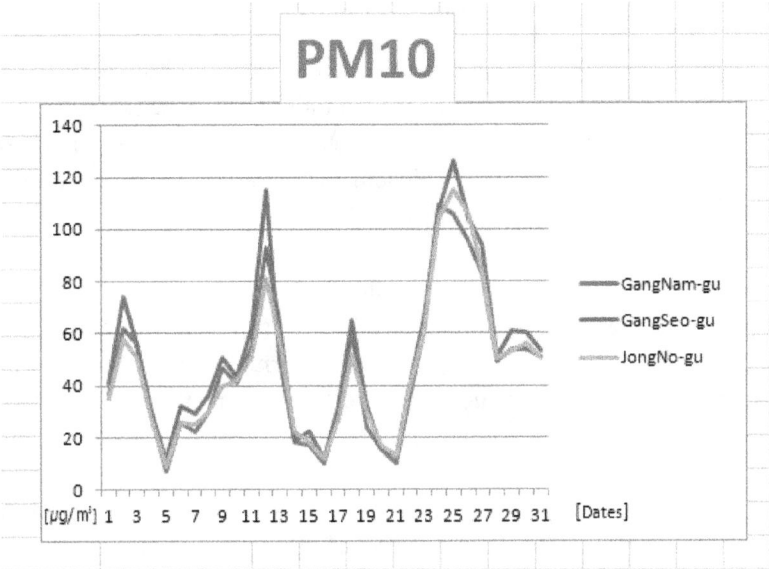

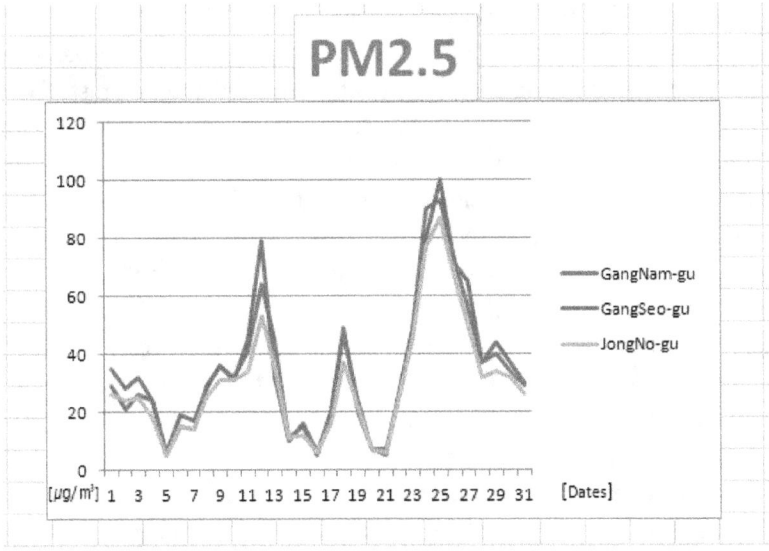

As a result of 70 percent of the interviews occurring during this period when the air pollution was most severe, memories of placing masks on their child, doctors' visits for pollutant related symptoms and using air purifiers were also fresh in the participant's memories causing them to reflect on how this affected their parenting perhaps more than they would have during another time of year.

The demographic match between the researcher and the participants is another variable which needs consideration when discussing potential limitations to the study. This has already been somewhat addressed in various chapters. As a thirty-six-year-old female Australian of European decent, married to a Korean, raising a three-and-a-half-year-old child in Korea at the time of writing, the researcher shared a number of demographic similarities with the participants. As described in the chapter devoted to methodology, the researcher was intentional in efforts to maintain reduction in the data collection and analysis process. Furthermore, as mentioned in the introduction, Creswell's phenomenological analysis method adapted from Moustakas begins with the researcher first describing their own experience of the phenomenon.[4] While admitting the impossibility of completely setting aside their experiences, the objective is to maintain focus on the participants' experiences and not the researcher's assumptions.[5]

Although at times similarities and differences between the researcher and participants' experiences were evident, there were also moments when the differences were just as notable. In addition, greater attention was given to how the experiences of the participants compared and contrasted with each other rather than with the researcher. This was an advantage of having the interviews clustered together in a relatively short period of time, as the responses of each of the participants were relatively fresh in the researcher's mind. The similarities between the researcher and the participant also facilitated a level of trust between the participant and researcher which perhaps would not have come as readily had there not been as many similarities. There was a trust birthed from the implicit belief that the researcher both understood and was sensitive to the intricacies of their unique experience which allowed for a deep level of sharing in the participant's responses. This was evidenced by the fact that some of the participants even allowed themselves to cry when they described some aspects of their experience such as loneliness and also the importance of passing on their cultural heritage to their children.

4. Creswell, *Qualitative Inquiry*, 193.
5. Creswell, *Qualitative Inquiry*, 193.

8.4 Opportunities for Further Study

While this research was significant in highlighting how deeply the Facebook social media groups are integrated into the expatriate mother's acculturation experience and creating "enclave communities" in particular, it has potential for further exploration. The implications of social media in contributing to feelings of isolation and loneliness, specifically as an expatriate, could be investigated further in other studies. A study conducted with women who were not a part of the online communities, perhaps comparing and contrasting participants with those who were, could give some insight into whether or not social media is actually beneficial to the acculturation process.

As outlined in the introduction, aside from Son's study, Anglophone women have not been researched as a distinct demographic apart from the larger trend of female marriage migration in Korea. As a result, detailed quantitative data outlining outcomes of childbirth, mental health, language challenges, and socioeconomic status specific to this demographic of marriage immigrants is not available. Subsequently, this study has attempted to contribute and make comparisons based on detailed qualitative experiences of Anglophone women from a relatively small sample base. In order to make comparisons in greater depth, more quantitative data about Anglophone women as a group needs to be gathered. There is the risk of this study contributing to a dichotomy of class stereotypes between Southeast Asian and Western marriage migrants which in reality is much more complex. Even so, perceptions of relatively higher socioeconomic status do contribute to the experience. Furthermore, broad comparisons can be made. There are certainly many instances where women from Southeast Asia meet, marry, and immigrate to Korea outside of commercialized marriage introduction services with motives other than hypogamy, particularly in more urban areas, but this is not reflective of the majority of the trend. In contrast, in the absence of a substantial economy facilitating marriage introductions between Anglophone women and Korean men, they are much more likely to meet through less formal interactions or introductions. Even in a generation of online dating applications and websites, the purpose of the introduction is less likely to be motivated primarily by desires to relocate to Korea. This is the case for the participants in this study.

In seeking participants, this study did not specifically seek those who had experienced acculturation stress. As a result, the experiences described by the participants, while detailing moments and histories of conflict, were a lot more established in their acculturation outcomes. This sample did however illustrate an awareness of the perception that they would be subject to more negative acculturation outcomes such as acculturation stress. More detailed case studies or narrative studies that go into deeper detail about instances of acculturation stress and narratives which contribute to coping strategies could be beneficial here. Ideally, this is also a unique time in Korean history where a longitudinal study of adaptive outcomes for multicultural families could be particularly revealing, in order to find more long-term mutually satisfying outcomes and policy solutions for both Korean society and marriage immigrants.

Appendix 1

INTERVIEW CONSENT FORM

Experiences of Expat, Intercultural Motherhood in Korea: A Qualitative Phenomenological Study

DEAR PARTICIPANT,

The following information is provided for you to decide whether you wish to participate in the present study. You should be aware that you are free to decide not to participate or to withdraw at any time without any obligation or burden.

The purpose of this study is to understand the experiences of international (particularly Anglophone) women residing and parenting in Korea with a Korean spouse. The procedure will be a single phenomenological study design. It is being conducted under the supervision of Professor Soo-Young Kwon (PhD) through Yonsei University.

Data collection will consist of a one-hour individual face-to-face interview (recorded and transcribed). Follow-up or clarification questions may be asked via email or phone messaging applications. The study may also include other materials which may help to further explore and clarify various themes as they emerge through the interviews, for example, photographic prompts and responses if deemed necessary by the researcher and participant.

Do not hesitate to ask any questions about the study either before participating or during the time that you are participating. I would be happy to share my findings with you after the research is completed. You may also be asked at some stage for feedback as to emerging themes during the data analysis stage of this study, however, your name will not be associated with the research findings in any way, and only the researcher will know your identity as a participant. Your privacy and confidentiality will be respected particularly if the study is submitted and accepted for publication in an academic journal or other medium.

There are no known risks and/or discomforts associated with this study. The expected benefits associated with your participation are the opportunity to participate in a qualitative research study and to provide a voice to bring awareness to the various experiences of international mothers in Korea.

Please sign your consent with full knowledge of the nature and purpose of the procedures. A copy of this consent form will be given to you to keep.

Date:
Signature of Participant:

Karen L. Kim
PhD Candidate
Yonsei University, Principal Investigator

Appendix 2

INTERVIEW PROTOCOL
Experiences of Expat,
Intercultural Motherhood in Korea

Time of Interview: _____

Date: _____

Place: _____

Interviewer: _____

Interviewee: _____

(Briefly describe the project)

Questions:

- Can you tell me about an experience you have had which defines or illustrates what it means for you to raise a multiracial child in Korea?

_____

_____

_____

_____

- How do you think your ideas or expectations of being a mother have changed or adapted while raising a child here in Korea?

  * Can you give some specific examples?

_____

_____

- What does the term "multicultural family" mean to you and your family?

_____

_____

_____

_____

- What are some of things that you consider to be advantages to raising your child here in Korea?

_____

_____

_____

_____

- What are some of your frustrations or difficulties in raising your child here in Korea?

_____

_____

_____

_____

- Do you have ways that you are actively trying to reconcile or counter-act these challenges?

_____

_____

_____

_____

- Is there anything else you would like to tell me about your journey and experience of becoming a mother in Korea?

_____

_____

_____

_____

BIBLIOGRAPHY

Abelmann, Nancy, and Hyunhee Kim. "A Failed Attempt at Transnational Marriage: Maternal Citizenship in a Globalizing South Korea." In *Cross-Border Marriages: Gender and Mobility in Transnational Asia*, edited by Nicole Constable, 101–23. Philadelphia: Pennsylvania, 2005.

Ahn, Ji-Hyun. "Global Migration and the Racial Project in Transition: Institutionalizing Racial Difference through the Discourse of Multiculturalism in South Korea." *Journal of Multicultural Discourses* 8.1 (2013) 29–47.

Augsburger, David W. *Pastoral Counseling Across Cultures*. Philadelphia: Westminster, 1986.

Beckett, Clare, and Marie Macey. "Race, Gender and Sexuality: The Oppression of Multiculturalism." *Women's Studies International Forum* 24.3 & 4 (2001) 309–19.

Bélanger, Danièle, et al. "Ethnic Diversity and Statistics in East Asia: 'Foreign Brides' Surveys in Taiwan and South Korea." *Ethnic and Racial Studies* 33.6 (2010) 1108–30.

Berry, John W. "Acculturation: Living Successfully in Two Cultures." *International Journal of Intercultural Relations* 29 (2005) 697–712.

Bornstein, Marc H. "The Specificity Principle in Acculturation Science." *Perspectives on Psychological Science* 12.1 (2017) 3–45.

Carroll R., M. Daniel. *Christians at the Border: Immigration, the Church and the Bible*. Grand Rapids: Baker Academic, 2008.

———. "Once a Stranger, Always a Stranger? Immigration, Assimilation and the Book of Ruth." *International Bulletin of Missionary Research* 39.4 (October 2015) 185–88.

Cawley, Kevin N. "Back to the Future: Recalibrating the Myth of Korea's Homogeneous Ethnicity." *Asian Ethnicity* 17.1 (2016) 150–60.

Cheng, Sealing. "Sexual Protection, Citizenship and Nationhood: Prostituted Women and Migrant Wives in South Korea." *Journal of Ethnic and Migration Studies* 37.10 (2011) 1627–48.

Choe, Hyun. "South Korean Society and Multicultural Citizenship." *Korea Journal* 47.4 (2007) 123–46.

Chosun Ilbo. "The Right Approach to Care for Multicultural Children." *The Chosun Ilbo*, November 30, 2009. http://english.chosun.com.

Chung, C. "Dual Citizenships among South Koreans Increasing." *The Korea Herald*, October 22, 2017. http://www.koreaherald.com.

Chung, Grace H., and Ji Young Lim. "Marriage Immigrant Mothers' Experience of Perceived Discrimination, Maternal Depression, Parenting Behaviors, and Adolescent Psychological Adjustment Among Multicultural Families in South Korea." *Journal of Child and Family Studies* 25 (2016) 2894–903.

Chung, Grace H., and Joan P. Yoo. "Using the Multicultural Family Support Centers and Adjustment among Interethnic and Interracial Families in South Korea." *Family Relations* 62 (February 2013) 241–53.

Constable, Nicole. *Romance of a Global Stage: Pen Pals, Virtual Ethnography and "Mail-Order" Marriages.* Berkeley: University of California Press, 2003.

Constable, Nicole, ed. *Cross Border Marriages: Gender and Mobility in Transnational Asia.* Philadelphia: Pennsylvania University Press, 2005.

Cooper-White, Pamela. *The Cry of Tamar: Violence against Women and the Church's Response.* Minneapolis: Fortress, 1995.

Creswell, John W. *Qualitative Inquiry and Research Design: Choosing Among Five Approaches.* 3rd ed. California: Sage, 2013.

Delaney, Robert F. "Voices of Foreign Brides: The Roots and Development of Multiculturalism in Korea [Book Review]." *Korean Studies* 38 (2014) 49–51.

Doehring, Carrie. "Developing Models of Feminist Pastoral Counseling." *The Journal of Pastoral Care* 46.1 (1992) 23–31.

———. "A Method of Feminist Pastoral Theology." In *Feminist Womanist Pastoral Theology*, edited by Bonnie J. Miller-McLemore and Brita Gill-Austern, 77–94. Nashville: Abingdon, 1999.

———. *The Practice of Pastoral Care: A Postmodern Approach.* Louisville: Westminster John Knox, 2006.

Fackler, Martin. "Baby Boom of Mixed Children Tests South Korea." *The New York Times*, November 29, 2009. http://www.nytimes.com.

Fortune, Marie M. *Sexual Violence: The Sin Revisited.* Ohio: Pilgrim, 2005.

Freeman, Caren. *Making and Faking Kinship: Marriage and Labor Migration between China and South Korea.* New York: Cornell University Press, 2011.

———. "Marrying Up and Marrying Down: The Paradoxes of Marital Mobility for Chosŏnjok Brides in South Korea." In *Cross-Border Marriages: Gender and Mobility in Transnational Asia*, edited by Nicole Constable, 80–100. Philadelphia: Pennsylvania, 2005.

Giorgi, Amedeo. "The Phenomenological Psychology of Learning and the Verbal Learning Tradition." In *Phenomenology Psychological Research*, edited by Amedeo Giorgi, 23–85. Pittsburgh: Duquesne University Press, 1985.

———. "Sketch of a Psychological Phenomenological Method." In *Phenomenology Psychological Research*, edited by Amedeo Giorgi, 8–22. Pittsburgh: Duquesne University Press, 1985.

Harvard Medical School Health. "Depression During Pregnancy and After" (September 2002), 6–8. www.health.harvard.edu.

Han, Geon-Soo. "Multicultural Korea: Celebration or Challenge of Multiethnic Shift in Contemporary Korea?" *Korea Journal* 47.4 (2007) 32–63.

Hurh, Gloria, ed. *We Married Koreans: Personal Stories of American Women with Korean Husbands.* Florida: Llumina, 2009.

Hwang, Jung-mee. "Positioning Migrant Mothers in a Multicultural Society: Realities, Discourse, and New Perspectives in Korea (Abstract)." *The Journal of Asian Women* 51.2 (2012) 141. [In Korean].

Bibliography

Im, Hyuk, et al. "Acculturation Stress and Mental Health Among the Marriage Migrant Women in Busan, South Korea." *Community Mental Health Journal* 30 (December 2013) 497–503.

Jäger, Siegfried, and Florentine Maier. "Theoretical and Methodological Aspects of Foucauldian Critical Discourse Analysis and Dispositive Analysis." In *Methods of Critical Discourse Analysis*, edited by Ruth Wodak and Michael Meyer, 33–61. 2nd ed. London: Sage, 2009.

Jones, Gavin, and Hsiu-hua Shen. "International Marriage in East and Southeast Asia: Trends and Research Emphases." *Citizenship Studies* 12.1 (2008) 9–25.

Jung, Hyunjoo. "Let Their Voices Be Seen: Exploring Mental Mapping as a Feminist Visual Methodology for the Study of Migrant Women." *International Journal of Urban and Regional Research* 38.3 (2014) 985–1002.

———. "Constructing Scales and Renegotiating Identities: Women Marriage Migrants in South Korea." *Asian and Pacific Migration Journal* 21.2 (2012) 193–215.

Kim, Agnes Davis. *I Married a Korean.* New York: The John Day Company, 1953.

Kim, Andrew Eungi. "Global Migration and South Korea: Foreign Workers, Foreign Brides and the Making of a Multicultural Society." *Ethnic and Racial Studies* 32.1 (2009) 70–92.

Kim, Bok-Lim C. "Marriages of Asian Women and American Military Men: The Impact of Gender and Culture." In *Re-visioning Family Therapy: Race, Culture, and Gender in Clinical Practice*, edited by Monica McGoldrick, 309–19. New York: Guilford, 1998.

Kim, Choong Soon. *Voices of Foreign Brides: The Roots and Development of Multiculturalism in Korea.* Lanham: Altamira, 2011.

Kim, Hyun Mee. "The State and Migrant Women: Diverging Hopes in the Making of 'Multicultural Families' in Contemporary Korea." *Korea Journal* 47.4 (2007) 100–122.

Kim, Hyuk-Rae, and Ingyu Oh. "Migration and Multicultural Contention in East Asia." *Journal of Ethnic and Migration Studies* 37.10 (2011) 1563–81.

Kim, Hyun-Sil. "Social Integration and Health Policy Issues for International Marriage Migrants Women in South Korea." *Public Health Nursing* 27.6 (2010) 561–70.

Kim, Jung A., et al. "Predictive Factors of Depression among Asian Female Marriage Immigrants in Korea." *Nursing and Health Sciences* 13 (2011) 275–81.

Kim, Junmo, et al. "Marriage Immigration and Gender in South Korea: Accounting for Gender Disparities in International Marriages." *Asia-Pacific Social Science Review* 12.2 (2012) 14–32.

Kim, Karen L. "Korea and the Gender Construction of Female Marriage Immigrants." *Pastoral Psychology* 66.1 (2017) 13–25.

Kim, Keuntae. "Cross-Border Marriages in South Korea and the Challenges of Rising Multiculturalism." *International Migration* 55.3 (2017) 74–88.

Kim, Lana, et al. "Toward Relationship-Directed Parenting: An Example of North American Born Second-Generation Korean-American Mothers and Their Partners." *Family Process* 53.1 (2014) 55–66.

Kim, Myung-Hye. "Changing Relationships between Daughters-in-Law and Mothers-in-Law in Urban South Korea." *Anthropological Quarterly* 69.4 (1996) 179–92.

Kim, Nora Hui-Jung. "Naturalizing Korean Ethnicity and Making 'Ethnic' Difference: A Comparison of North Korean Settlement and Foreign Bride Incorporation Policies in South Korea." *Asian Ethnicity* 17.2 (2016) 185–98.

Bibliography

Kim, Soon-Yang, and Yeong-Gyun Shin. "Immigrant Brides in the Korean Rural Farming Sector: Social Exclusion and Policy Responses." *Korean Observer* 39.1 (2008) 1–35.

Kim, Young Jeong. "Daughters-in-Law of Korea?" Policies and Discourse on Migration in South Korea." WP-11-92. University of Oxford: Center on Migration, Policy and Society, 2011. http://www.compas.ox.ac.uk/2011/wp-2011-092-kim_policies_migration_korea/.

Kim, Yugyun, et al. "Don't Ask for Fair Treatment? A Gender Analysis of Ethnic Discrimination, Response to Discrimination, and Self-Rated Health among Marriage Migrants in South Korea." *International Journal for Equity in Health* 15.112 (2016) 1–9.

The Korean Ministry of Environment (MOE) and The Korean Environment Corporation (KECO). *Air Korea.* http://www.airkorea.or.kr.

Lan, Pei-Chia. "'They Have More Money But I Speak Better English!' Transnational Encounters between Filipina Domestics and Taiwanese Employers." *Identities: Global Studies in Culture and Power* 10.2 (2003) 133–61.

Lee, Hyonuk. "Trafficking in Women? Or Multicultural Family? The Contextual Difference of Commodification of Intimacy." *Gender, Place and Culture* 21.10 (2014) 1249–66.

Lee, Mary. "Mixed Race Peoples in the Korean National Imaginary and Family." *Korean Studies* 32 (2008) 56–85.

Lee, Yean-Ju, et al. "International Marriages in South Korea: The Significance of Nationality and Ethnicity." *Journal of Population Research* 23.2 (2006) 165–82.

Lee, Yeong-mee. "Ruth and Marriage Migrant Women in Korea." *Madang* 18 (December 2012), 115–32.

Leslie, Kristen J. *When Violence is No Stranger: Pastoral Counseling with Survivors of Acquaintance Rape.* Minneapolis: Fortress, 2003.

Lim, Timothy. "Rethinking Belongingness in Korea: Transnational Migration, 'Migrant Marriages' and the Politics of Multiculturalism." *Pacific Affairs* 83.1 (2010) 51–71.

Mann, Jatinder. "The Introduction of Multiculturalism in Canada and Australia, 1960s–1970s." *Nations and Nationalism* 18.3 (2012) 483–503.

Miller-McLemore, Bonnie J. *Also a Mother: Work and Family as Theological Dilemma.* Nashville: Abingdon, 1994.

———. "Feminist Theory in Pastoral Theology." In *Feminist Womanist Pastoral Theology,* edited by Bonnie J. Miller-McLemore and Brita Gill-Austern, 77–94. Nashville: Abingdon, 1999.

Min, Dong-yong. "Karen Kim's Uncommon Life as the Mistress of the Head Family of an Ancient Noble Clan." *Dong-a Ilbo Korea Focus,* September 17, 2011. http.//www.donga.com.

Ng, Ting Kin, et al. "Acculturation and Cross-Cultural Adaption: The Moderating Role of Social Support." *International Journal of International Relations* 59 (2017) 19–30.

Oh, Joong-Hwan, et al. "Asian Cultural Collectivism, Acculturation, and Life Satisfaction among Ethnic Asian Brides in South Korea." *Asian Women* 30.3 (2014) 23–56.

Park, Chisung, et al. "The Formation of Social Constructions of Female Marriage Migrants and Female Work Migrants in South Korea." *Asian Women* 29.4 (2013) 107–40.

Robinson, Kathryn. "Marriage Migration, Gender Transformations, and Family Values in the 'Global Ecumene.'" *Gender, Place and Culture* 14.4 (2007) 483–97.

Son, Sarah. "National Identity and Social Integration in Cross Border Marriages Between Anglophone Women and Korean Men: When Love and Culture Clash." *Asian Survey* 59.4 (2019) 630–52.

Bibliography

Statistics Korea. "Marriage and Divorce Statistics in 2015" (April 7, 2016). http://kostat. go.kr.

Statistics Korea. "Status of Marriage Migrant by Nationality/Region" (August 18, 2017). http://kosis.kr.

Statistics Korea. "Vital Statistics in February 2018" (April 25, 2018). http://kostat.go.kr.

Statistics Korea. "Vital Statistics of Immigrants in 2014" (November 19, 2015). http:// kostat.go.kr.

Tanner, Kathryn. *Theories of Culture: A New Agenda for Theology*. Minneapolis: Fortress, 1997.

Trible, Phyllis. *God and the Rhetoric of Sexuality*. Philadelphia: Fortress, 1978.

Ward, Colleen, and Larissa Kus. "Back To and Beyond Berry's Basics: The Conceptualization, Operationalization and Classification of Acculturation." *International Journal of Intercultural Relations* 36 (2012) 472–85.

Washbrook, Elizabeth, et al. "The Development of Young Children of Immigrants in Australia, Canada, the United Kingdom, and the United States." *Child Development* 83.5 (2012) 1591–607.

Webb, Barry G. *Five Festival Garments: Christian Reflections on The Song of Songs, Ruth, Lamentations, Ecclesiastes, Esther*. Illinois: Intervarsity, 2000.

Wodak, Ruth, and Michael Meyer. "Critical Discourse Analysis: History, Agenda, Theory and Methodology." In *Methods of Critical Discourse Analysis*, edited by Ruth Wodak and Michael Meyer, 1–33. 2nd ed. London: Sage, 2009.

Won, Seojin, and Hyemee Kim. "Importance of Family Values Differences Between Husbands and Wives in Determining Depression in Foreign Wives in Korean Multicultural Families." *Asian Social Work and Policy Review* 8 (2014) 1–15.

Yang, Hyunah. "'Multicultural Families' in South Korea: A Socio-Legal Approach." *North Carolina Journal of International Law and Commercial Regulation* 37.1 (2011) 47–81.

Zhang, Yuanting, and Jennifer Van Hook. "Marital Dissolution Among Interracial Couples." *Journal of Marriage and Family* 71.1 (2009) 95–107.